Sarah Tytler, J. L. Watson

The Songstresses of Scotland

Sarah Tytler, J. L. Watson

The Songstresses of Scotland

ISBN/EAN: 9783741179204

Manufactured in Europe, USA, Canada, Australia, Japa

Cover: Foto ©Andreas Hilbeck / pixelio.de

Manufactured and distributed by brebook publishing software (www.brebook.com)

Sarah Tytler, J. L. Watson

The Songstresses of Scotland

THE SONGSTRESSES OF SCOTLAND

By SARAH TYTLER and J. L. WATSON

TWO VOLS.—II.

STRAHAN & CO., PUBLISHERS
56 LUDGATE HILL, LONDON
1871

CONTENTS OF VOL. II.

	PAGE
LADY ANNE BARNARD (1750—1825)	1
CAROLINA BARONESS NAIRNE (1766—1845)	108
MISS JOANNA BAILLIE (1762—1851)	180

LADY ANNE BARNARD.

1750—1825.

LADY ANNE BARNARD came of one of the most lordly lines in Scotland. On the Lindsays' side she was descended from the bold barons of Crawford, Spynie, and Balcarres. Reckoning by both sides of the house, she was "the daughter of a hundred earls."

Her birth at Balcarres in 1750 had been looked forward to by the Jacobites as the fulfilment of a prophecy, that the first child of the last descendant of so loyal a house would restore the exiled Stuarts. But, as Lady Anne herself records with great glee, wizards, witches, bards, fortune-tellers, and old ladies were covered with confusion by the arrival of a daughter—only a daughter—at what the Lindsays were fond of calling the *château*, which had been rendered poverty-stricken by fines and forfeitures.

The country-seat of Balcarres, that proved so wonderfully capacious in after years when Mistress Cockburn was one of its occupants, was very old-fashioned. It was situated not very far from that succession of Dutch-like towns on the Fife coast which, before their prosperity fell under the death-blow of the Union, one of the King Jamies had sharply characterised as "a golden fringe to a beggar's mantle." But the beggar's mantle part of the comparison was hardly fair to the sheltered and cultivated strath which extended from Largo Bay to the East Neuk. Balcarres lay midway in the strath, backed by its Craig and the Hill of Rires, and facing the sea frith which brought "the wind of God" fresh from the German Ocean. Between the nest of the Lindsays and the bare coast, there basked in the sunshine, and cowered a little in the keen frost of the region, farms and woods, a blue loch, and two drowsy hamlets. In the west, with the sun setting behind it, was the green sandy

Law of Largo, out of the shadow of which Sir Andrew Wood had sailed his yellow carvel and cleared the frith of English boats. In the east was the round hummock of Kelly Law. Close to this was the castle of the musical Earl of Kelly—the early home of Lady Betty, Lady Ann, and Lady Christian Erskine, good friends and neighbours of the Lindsays. A little nearer stood the quaint, steep little village and exquisite church of St. Monans, with Balcaskie House and Newark Castle, where, after the '15, Earl James of Balcarres had been hidden by the aid of one of the young ladies of the Anstruther family. Another Anstruther, Sir John, of Elie House, married, in the same year that Lady Anne Barnard was born, the famous beauty and wit, Jenny Faa, a daughter of the gipsy merchant of Dunbar. Between Balcarres and Elie were the village, the estate, and the house of Kinneuchar, on their Loch Bethune, the laird of which having been present at a public dinner and compelled to drink as a toast the health of William, Duke of Cumberland, rose up and proposed the health of Sibbald, the butcher in Colinsburgh, swearing that as he had drunk his friends' butcher, they should drink his butcher. Farther off, in the Largo direction, was the white house on the hill of the Grange, the lairds of which, the Malcolms, had been once and again humble allies of the Lindsays—a Malcolm having been with Earl Alexander in Holland, and another (whose wife, herself an earl's daughter, had supported his family by spinning and selling thread in his absence) with Earl James at St. Germain.

Lady Anne, like Lady Grisell Baillie, was the eldest of many children; and, like Miss Jean Elliot, she belonged to a family whose literary bent was as ancient as the days of Sir David of the Mount and of "old Pittscottie." Earl James, Lady Anne's father, having himself written a history of his house, laid on his family the injunction that a son or a daughter in each generation should carry on the record. A pleasant fruit of this injunction survives in Lady Anne's sketches of her youth and of the friends by whom she was surrounded. These sketches are included in the "Lives of the Lindsays."

Earl James, who died at seventy-seven, when his eldest daughter was seventeen years of age, had seen service both by sea and land; but his own and his father's share in the '15 spoilt his promotion. He was grey and gaunt, somewhat of a Baron Bradwardine, though more accomplished than learned. In his brigadier wig and gouty shoe he lost his heart at Moffatt to fat, fair, severely sensible Miss Dalrymple, who in her twenty-third year was nearly young enough to have been his grand-daughter. The Earl proposed, Miss Dalrymple said nay. The Earl, more or less of an invalid all his life, fell sicker than usual under his disappointment, and made his will. Having no near relations, with great dignity and magnanimity he left his obdurate mistress half his slender fortune. But the Earl did not die then; and Miss Dalrymple, hearing of the deed, was smitten to the heart, and became the energetic Countess, the over-anxious, imperious mother of eleven spirited children. The eight sons and the three daughters were no sinecure of a charge even to so strict a disciplinarian as the buxom, blooming Countess. They were for ever breaking out of nurseries and school-rooms to commit raids in the domains of Mammy Bell, the old housekeeper; often carrying the war into the garden or the offices. The Countess would inflict chastisements, not by proxy, but with her own little white hand, which, as Lady Anne bore testimony, could strike hard. Lady Balcarres found variety in her subjects; and some of them were stiff-necked enough. "Oh, my lady, my lady!" cried Robert, plain and practical always, "whip me and let me go if you please." Her little son John, who lived to be the prisoner of Hyder Ali in Seringapatam, told Lady Balcarres, when she took a plaything from him because of a fault, "Woman, I told you I would do the same thing, and I'll do the same to-morrow again." To-morrow came, and he kept his word. He was whipped, and another plaything withdrawn; but the sun shone warm: "Ah!" said he, "here is a fine day; my mother cannot take *it* from me."

Lady Balcarres led her children no easy life in return for their contumacy. What with whipping, imprisonment in dark closets, fasting, and doses of rhubarb administered impartially to all the culprits, according to their offences—from tearing of frocks and breeches to running away—the Countess did not shirk her duty.

"Odsfish, madam!" remonstrated the worthy old Earl, "you will break the spirits of my young troops. I will not have it so."

But no spirits were broken where earnestness and affection formed the foundation of the despotism. , Little, blue-eyed, golden-haired Lady Margaret, who had the precocious infirmity of sighing and hanging her cherub head in her nursery because nobody loved her, was cured for the time of her morbid pining. As for generous, joyous Lady Anne—the "sister Anne" and "Annie" of that great circle—she was the hardest to punish of them all; for she ate and drank bread and water with complete philosophy, and would ask the butler to give her a bit of oat-cake out of mere pleasure in the change.

The healthy Spartan children had many pleasures which are out of the reach of their daintily-bred brothers and sisters of to-day.

These old Balcarres children were allowed a large amount of personal freedom in rambling and scrambling. They could wade in the burn which flowed through Balcarres Den; the sisters in tucked-up yellow and silver silk frocks with gauze flounces, manufactured, to suit the children's needs, out of part of the marriage finery of Lady Balcarres. They could pay daily visits to the farm-yard, looking in on their familiar friends of oxen, swine, and pigeons. They could sit on lazy cows' backs, devouring turnips for the sitters' own share, and scattering grain to obsequious cocks and hens. They had a Sunday rest from all tasks, save the repetition of so many verses of a psalm and attendance at the parish kirk; and they had a Sunday dinner at my lord's and my lady's table, winding up with a fatherly treat of sweetmeats.

The solid rudiments of knowledge were imparted alike to boys and girls by a reverend and absent-minded tutor. The airy superstructure of womanly accomplishments in Ladies Anne, Margaret, and Elizabeth was reared by the most fantastic of indigent gentlewomen, "the least

little woman that ever was seen for nothing,"—
Henrietta Cumming. Not only as Lady Anne's
governess, but as the "Sylph," and favoured
"Hen," "Henny," and "Hennifie," of Mistress
Cockburn's correspondence, this curious little
lady deserves yet another paragraph.

She was found by Lady Balcarres weeping
and painting butterflies in the garret of an
Edinburgh lodging-house, which was kept
by her aunt. She had persuaded herself
of her descent from the Red Comyn himself, and was possibly brought to Balcarres
partly as a speculation, partly as an act of
charity. Henrietta sang sweetly, wrote letters
which Mistress Cockburn compared, for want
of another simile, to the letters of Rousseau,
and worked, as has been recorded, at mantua-
making, millinery, and ruffles, for which she
could draw elegant designs in flowers and
birds. The Countess had thoughts of setting
the reduced lady to instruct her daughters
in these branches, and causing her to mess with
my lady's maid, whose origin was doubtless no
lower than that of a country manse or parish

school-house. But Henrietta turned the tables on the strong-willed Countess. By lavish tears and persistent starvation, she found her way to the family dinner-table. By her opposition to what she called Lady Balcarres' "haughty and unprovoked misrepresentation" of the act of friendship by which she condescended to teach the little ladies, and her spurning of a salary, she established herself for half a lifetime in Lord Balcarres' crowded household on terms of comparative equality. Not only so; she got from the good, burdened man a legacy on his death, and what was more unjustifiable, procured, through his influence, during his life, a pension from Government. Henrietta's pride, which would not let her take wages for her work, did not prevent her from accepting public alms to which she does not seem to have had the shadow of a title, unless in the fact that she painted a gown for Queen Charlotte. Yet the little woman, sharp-tongued when she could let her tongue out, was one of those characters in whom the falseness, supposing she proved herself false, and the truth were about equally balanced. They deceive themselves almost as much as they deceive others. She was not only fascinating, because she was pretty and clever, and possessed a simplicity as real as it was affected, but in the midst of her calculating worldliness, and in defiance of it, she could be magnanimous, and was devotedly attached to her friends.

Although Henrietta's offices were detrimental in some respects, she shared in full the Lindsays' love of letters. She was capable of at least joining the two elder sisters in their voyages of discovery in the old library, where, according to Lady Anne, they had leave "to drive through the sea of books without pilot or rudder." The girls were free to lug down whatever musty volumes took their fancy. The desultory knowledge and accomplishments which they thus acquired were remarkable. It is as if the old Lindsays had found a "royal road to mathematics." This is proved when we sing Lady Anne's ballad, and read her letters, and hear how Lady Margaret translated Bürger's "Leonore" in fair verse, while Lady Elizabeth did the same service for Tasso's "Gerusalemme Liberata."

Lady Anne was old enough to be her father's companion by the time that Lord Cummerland, the son and heir, had finished his studies at St. Andrew's University, and the Honourables Robert, Colin, James, William, Charles, John, and Hugh were being sent, in the earlier relays, to attend the college in Edinburgh, prior to becoming "a family of soldiers." Lady Anne was the Earl's amused young associate in his self-imposed obligation of compiling the family chronicles. One of her earliest recollections was seeing him receive a huge bundle of papers, wrapped in a plaid, from the Laird of Macfarlane, the ugliest chieftain, with the reddest nose, whom the child had ever seen.

Lady Anne is said to have imbibed her father's disposition, and she certainly profited by his honourable, shrewd, yet fond advice to his two girls, who were of an age to understand him. He counselled them to be good and mild, cheerful and complaisant. He told them that men loved such companions as could help to make them gay and easy; and for this end fair nymphs should provide chains as well as nets in order to secure victims as well as acquire them. He bade them have the Muses as well as the Graces to aid Nature, which had been very good to his "Annie" and his "dear Peg" (budding beauties and wits of sixteen and fourteen). After insisting on the advantages of music, and of the Italian language in the service of music, and after urging the claims of books and religion, he declared that as much of philosophy as concerned the moral virtues would help to make them happy, even if they were "condemned" to be old maids. If they became wives, he urged them to be amiable. This was the best instrument for gaining power, as their husbands would have more pleasure in pleasing them than in pleasing themselves. Finally, he held up for the example of his daughters the two traditionary models of virtuous womanhood among the Lindsays—Earl James's respected aunt, Lady Sophia, and his dear sister, Lady Betty—declaring with faith, which was touching in its child-likeness, "whom I wish to embrace you kindly in another world when you have had enough of this." As a fitting commentary on their old father's advice, Lady Anne and Lady Margaret were daily witnesses of his tender gallantry towards their mother, which was but the quintessence of his tender gallantry towards all women. He delighted to ride across the country, bearing a busy dame's commissions. Having on one occasion caught an old woman, his pensioner, in the act of helping herself to his cherished turnips, he scolded her hotly for the liberty, receiving no answer but her curtseys. When she did speak she made the audacious request, "Eh! my lord, they're unco heavy; will ye no gie me a lift?" and he followed up his scolding by hoisting the sack on her back.

But a multitude of influences helped to mould young Lady Anne. The Balcarres of her day was rich in inhabitants. It could muster fifty members of its own household at a ball, and its household was peculiarly rich in character. Old Lady Dalrymple, the children's grandmother, was comparatively of a soft and sleepy order of womankind. In her own house in Edinburgh she came down every morning in search of the key which hung upon her finger. But very different was Miss Soph Johnstone, whose rough voice sung at its highest pitch—

> "Eh, quo' the lod, it's a braw licht nicht,
> The wind's in the west, and the mune shines bricht."

The clatter of the private forge she had erected in her bed-room, the caw of the rooks, and the gurgle of the shattered and repaired Venus *jet d'eau* in the garden, were the notable sounds on a quiet day at old Balcarres. Soph, the Laird of Hilton's daughter, came to pay a visit to Lady Balcarres on her marriage. She remained for thirteen years, taking up in succession each child till it was out of long clothes. She was only true to her first love in the person of Lady Anne. But Soph's partisanship was a fatal distinction. Lady Anne's admission to the sanctum of the forge, and her installation into the mysteries of fancy horseshoe-making, awoke Henrietta Cumming's jealous resentment, and alienated the governess entirely from her eldest pupil. There was an inevitable enmity between rude, fierce Soph Johnstone, and suave, capricious Henrietta Cumming. Lady Anne's first exercise of tact was in trying to maintain peace between the two belligerents, and to make them both happy. For it was the necessity of a gay, pleasure-loving nature, even in girlhood, to have all around her happy. It remains to the credit of Lady Anne that from youth to age she spared no trouble and grudged no pains for this end, and that she was in general as incapable of bearing malice against her neighbours as of fancying herself slighted by them. But this satisfaction in the contentment of her fellow-creatures did not prevent her from playing mischievous pranks on them, especially when she was instigated and backed by her trusty ally, Lady Margaret. One of their worst tricks was their writing and forwarding a letter, purporting to be from a rich cousin who had lately returned from abroad, to no less a person than Soph Johnstone, soliciting her company for a long visit. Miss Soph was completely deceived. She wrote and despatched a letter of acceptance, gave out her clothes to be mended, ordered a new wig, and explained to her young friends, with a certain sober softening down of her eccentricities, the motives of her departure. The giddy girls stood aghast at what they had done; and the consequences of their escapade frightened them out of such practical joking. There arose upon them a late sense of the piteous contrast between their own circumstances and those of their victim. Before she should have dismantled her forge, they rushed to her room with a full confession of their delinquency, and made earnest promises not to offend in a like manner again. Throwing themselves on Soph's masculine scorn of anything like petty recrimination, and relying on her bark being worse than her bite for all young people's folly, they experienced clemency at her hand.

Lady Anne in her youth was not confined to Balcarres. The rock of the Bass, which resembled "a huge whale" rising out of the water opposite the *château* windows, was hardly the most suggestive object in the sweep of the frith. Dancing eyes, with plenty of speculation in them, would often wander in the direction of the ferry of Kinghorn. Beyond the ferry lay Edinburgh, the metropolis, where the Lindsays had not only an indulgent grandmother, but hosts of cousins and allies. Among those kinsmen and friends, "Annie," "sister Anne," "charming Lady Anne," with her instinctive *savoir-faire*, her good-humour, and overbrimming fun and feeling, must have been immensely popular. The Lindsays, on their side, were strongly drawn to their cousins, when, in the end, Cummerland married a Dalrymple, and Robert a Dick.

An aunt of Lady Anne's, a figure more picturesque than engaging, lived in the Lawnmarket, where Burns had his lodging. This was the Dowager Countess of Balcarres, Margaret of Scotstarvet, who had the blood of the wizard of Balweary in her veins. A scantily provided-for widow, she hoarded her jointure to relieve the embarrassments of her husband's brother's children. She used to walk out, in order to visit the younger Lady Balcarres, dressed in a large black silk bonnet projecting over her face, a black gown, and a white apron. She always carried a staff in her hand.

A favourite haunt of Lady Anne's was the old Earl of Selkirk's house in Hyndford Place, which was then occupied by Dr. Rutherfurd, Sir Walter Scott's grandfather. Lady Anne played on the Misses Rutherfurds' harpsichord, and sang her ballads to the accompaniment. Behind the screen, with the harlequin and columbine, Lady Anne chatted with her cronies— the Misses Rutherfurd, and Miss Hepburn of Congalton. Miss Jeanie Rutherfurd boasted to Lady Anne of the wonderful bairn, her nephew in George Square.

At the assemblies, when Lady Margaret was selected to dance in the Beauty set, Lady Anne would by no means decline on that account to stand up next in the Heartsome set; while both the sisters might figure together in the Maiden set.

The theatre was a resort of the Lindsays. Its audience was then so aristocratic, and the members so well known to each other, that it presented many of the features of a county gathering. Thus, when Lord Balcarres died, as Mistress Cockburn wrote, the news of my lord's death thinned the play-house till after the funeral. Lady Anne must have improved scores of opportunities of "crying her eyes out" over *Jane Shore* and *The Gamester*, and of "laughing till she was fit to drop" at *The Provoked Husband* and *The Beaux' Stratagem*.

In her own home, at assembly or play-house, Lady Anne could scarcely have helped coming across a quiet, middle-aged woman of her own rank, and a family connection—Miss Jean Elliot —although it was not till long years afterwards that the apparently sober-minded woman was found guilty of writing an extremely romantic and doleful ballad.

Notwithstanding the natural attractions of Edinburgh, the Lindsays were judiciously taught to consider that no spot on earth had superior attractions to Balcarres, and that no reasonable being ought to be other than perfectly happy there. The extremely low condition of the family purse rendered it impossible that they could take frequent excursions, even within the modest limits of driving twenty miles in the Balcarres coach to the Kinghorn ferry, and of hiring a pinnace, and having themselves rowed across the tossing barrier. It might be one great secret of the success of these Lindsays that they early learnt self-denial, and that they stood shoulder to shoulder throughout their history. Lord Cummerland, living on his pay, supplemented his brothers' and sisters' allowances. The Honourable Robert bestowed the gains arising from his trading, in a gift of fifteen hundred pounds, to purchase his brother James's majority, and employed any sums realised by him in England in helping to pay off the debt on the Balcarres estate.

The Lindsays trace their descent from a Norman line. Their "lightness" is French, and so is their form of family affectionateness, with its power of accommodating itself to varying tastes and tempers, from youth to age. One hears of the hereditary reddish-golden hair, and that too can be proved to be Norman—of the purest water. Lady Margaret, the beauty of

Lady Anne's generation, had the golden hair, the eyes of "heavenly blue," the dazzling fairness of skin, the Grecian nose, and the fine turn of the head and throat, on which her elder sister lovingly enlarges. It would seem that Lady Anne bore more resemblance to the Lindsay who was her immediate predecessor, the gay but gaunt earl. If, however, she was not beautiful, she was very elegant and graceful, with all the "presence," animation, and piquancy which are the most irresistible weapons of many a high-bred belle.

As beauties are given to marry, Lady Margaret at the age of eighteen, married Mr. Fordyce of Roehampton, and went with him to England. Lady Anne, two years older, missed her sister's presence much. She tried to fill up the blank in her life at Balcarres by scribbling prose and verse on the covers of old letters. Her little room up the steep winding stair commanded a view of the loch and the frith, and she was now often occupied in it. In these circumstances, as she wrote long afterwards to Sir Walter Scott, she composed "Auld Robin Gray."

There was an old Scotch air (not, however, the air to which the song is now sung, for that we owe to an English clergyman) of which Lady Anne was very fond, and which Soph Johnstone was in the habit of singing to words which were far from choice. It struck Lady Anne that she could supply the air with a tale of virtuous distress in humble life, with which all could sympathise. Robin Gray was the name of a shepherd at Balcarres, who was familiar to the children of the house. He had once arrested them in their flight to an indulgent neighbour's. Lady Anne revenged this arrest by seizing the old man's name, and preventing it from passing into forgetfulness. While she was in the act of heaping misfortunes on the heroine Jeanie, her sister Elizabeth, twelve or thirteen years her junior, strayed into the little room, and saw "sister Anne" at her escritoire.

"I have been writing a ballad, my dear," the frank elder sister told her little confidante; "and I am oppressing my heroine with many misfortunes. I have already sent her Jamie to sea, broken her father's arm, and made her mother fall sick, and given her auld Robin for a lover, but I wish to load her with a fifth sorrow in the four lines. Help me to one, I pray."

"Steal the cow, sister Anne," said the little Elizabeth.

The cow was immediately lifted, and the song completed.

"Auld Robin Gray" at once became popular at Balcarres and in the neighbourhood; but Lady Anne's authorship was only known to the immediate members of her family. In spite of her resolution to be silent on the question, she had sometimes difficulty in escaping detection. After singing "Auld Robin Gray" at Dalkeith, Lady Jane Scott, the Duke of Buccleuch's sister, said to her that she sang the song as if she had written it herself, and declared that if Lady Anne would not bribe her by a copy she would betray the secret. Lady Anne's ultimate explanation of her reticence was, that she dreaded to be known as a writer, because those who did not write would become shy of her. It was an innate feeling of Lady

Anne's that she had rather confer pleasure than inspire awe. When the outer world took up the song and made much of it, a reward of twenty guineas was offered for information as to its source, and the period to which it belonged; the Society of Antiquaries thinking the subject worth investigation. Lady Anne, more from hauteur and a spirit of merry mischief than from any other feeling, held curiosity at arm's length, and baffled all investigation. Her best reward was seeing a company of dancing dogs act the little drama below her windows.

Lady Margaret was to fare worse than her brothers—worse than any of them, although the young midshipman William was drowned off St. Helena in 177—, and Captain James was struck by grape-shot in storming the redoubts of Cuddalore, and died of his wound in a French hospital in 1783. Light compared with hers were the sufferings of Captain John, who was taken prisoner by Hyder Ali's forces in the battle of Conjeveram in 1780, and lay in irons at Seringapatam, where he and his friend

Captain Baird may have lightened their terrible captivity, which lasted three years, by talk of home and half-forgetful laughter over the eccentricities of their old friend, David Baird's aunt, Miss Soph Johnstone. The ills of the brothers were those of the body rather than of the soul; and those even of Captain John were short compared with Lady Margaret's. Before she had attained her nineteenth year, her husband had ruined and disgraced himself. Her letters to him contain nothing but resignation and tenderness. By the time she was twenty-two, she had to pay a farewell visit to her beautiful bridal home in order to choose from that which had been hers what she was able to re-purchase. "I prayed for a little rain to sadden the glories of the prospect to a more suitable gloominess," she wrote to Lady Anne. But her prayer was not granted: the day was delightful; the place in perfect order; and every tree and shrub flourishing. She could only give a parting look, peep at the cartoons and the great room, and step into the carriage, carrying with her "a bunch of roses."

When Mr. Fordyce died within a few years, Lady Anne went up to London, and joined Lady Margaret (who was a childless widow) in Berkeley Square. Here the two sisters lived together between fifteen and twenty years. The great world of London was different from what was even then rapidly becoming the provincial world of Edinburgh. The Countess of Balcarres was wont to excuse herself jestingly for not dwelling with her daughters on the plea that she was nobody in England. But the sisters Lindsay were somebody in London. The beauty, modesty, and intellectual refinement of the young widow, Lady Margaret Fordyce, and the spirit and genius of Lady Anne Lindsay, were not such common qualities that they should have been lost in a crowd. In time, the little Lady Elizabeth of the sisters' early memories married happily the accomplished Earl of Hardwicke. The Honourable John Lindsay, in consolation for his sufferings, was to take from the congenially witty and lettered house of North a wife of whom Sir Walter Scott remarked that she never opened her mouth without reminding him of the princess who could not comb her locks without scattering abroad pearls and rubies. This sister-in-law served, without any other bond of union, to bring Lady Anne and Lady Margaret *en rapport* with the Guildford set, including Horace Walpole, the Ailesburys, and the Berrys.

Burke and Wyndham, who had so petted "little Burney," were familiar friends of the sisters in Berkeley Square; and so were Sheridan and Dundas. The Prince Regent himself, whose inclinations tended in general less worthily, was capable of being a princely friend in this instance. He was especially attracted by "sister Anne," as he too chose to call her. On one occasion when he was ill he sent for her to cheer him, and to receive from him a gold chain as a token of his regard, because he might never see her again. The Lindsays, whose loyalty was a passion which no suffering could cool, valued to the utmost the Regent's good-will.

Lady Anne and Lady Margaret, with Lady Charlotte North and the Guildfords, must have made the pilgrimage, customary with pilgrims in their rank, to Strawberry Hill, and been courteously treated by its old fine-lady master.

No doubt the book-loving sisters indulged in an early perusal of Cowper's "Task," and joined in the nine days' wonder at Darwin's "Botanic Garden." Very likely they had some acquaintance with Hannah More, who frequently visited London, making her head-quarters with Bishop Porteus, meeting Horace Walpole at Garrick's widow's, and writing her "Religion of the Fashionable World." Mrs. Carter, the translator of Epictetus, was likewise of the great world, and was in the way of ladies who did not dream of going out of their way to seek literary merit.

Breaking in upon their grief for the brothers they had lost, and their anxiety regarding that other brother whose fate remained for a time uncertain, Lady Anne and Lady Margaret would hear the declaration of the Independence of America, where some of the Lindsays had fought; and they would read of the killing of Captain Cook, and of the death of Charles Edward. As Londoners of the period, they

would have the full benefit of the Popish riots
and of the trial of Warren Hastings. With the
spice of malice that marked the rest of the
quality in the matter, Ladies Anne and
Margaret were sure to enter into the last
enterprise of an Irish Gunning, when the
niece of the famous beauties, after the great
fortunes of the house were on the wane, ventured on the bold but unsuccessful stroke of
maintaining, to the Marquis of Blandford's
blank astonishment, that he had made her an
offer of marriage. On account of Mrs. Piozzi's
daughter, Queeny, who had become one of themselves, a Scotch earl's popular sisters might consent to grace the *fêtes* still given at Streatham,
but which had sadly fallen off, like their rash
mistress. If so, the visitors would learn from
Mrs. Piozzi all that she had done in Mr. Thrale's
lifetime for the Doctor, and how small the great
man had shown himself to her in the end. The
members of the Balcarres family must have
witnessed with intelligent delight the playing
of John Kemble and Liston, of Sarah Siddons,
Miss Farren, and Mrs. Jordan.

By 1789 Lord Balcarres had married his cousin, Miss Dalrymple, who, through her mother, was heiress of Haigh Hall, in Lancashire; and while he was with his regiment, "young Lady Bal" was in Edinburgh for the education of her children. The Honourable Robert Lindsay had returned from India, and was celebrating his marriage with another cousin—pretty, domestic Miss Betsy Dick of Prestonfield. Before he had left Scotland, "he had marked her for his own" while she was yet a child. He had not only bought the estate of Leuchars, in Fife, but had settled annuities on his mother, Countess Anne, and on his sister, Lady Margaret. Countess Anne had removed to Edinburgh, and settled there with her cousin, dear friend, and protector, whom she thenceforth styled her "husband" —Mrs. Anne Murray Keith. Their house was in George Square, and opposite that of young Lady Bal, whose carriage and horses were at the command of the old ladies. They found themselves in the very centre of kindred and friends more numerous than often fall to the lot even of men and women who have done well for themselves.

The Countess's house in George Square, to which Lady Anne came on visits, has been lovingly described by Mrs. Gillespie Smyth, daughter of Ambassador Keith. It had its snug parlour profusely adorned with family pictures. Books loaded the tables, the place of honour being assigned to the Bible and the Book of Common Prayer. Next to them stood a well-bound, well-thumbed Shakespeare, volumes of English divines, and a copy of Dryden's Fables, "opening of itself at 'The Flower and the Leaf.'" Politics and history, in which the mistresses of the house had always regarded themselves as deeply concerned, had their oracles. French literature was represented by La Fontaine's Fables (great favourites of Earl James's), "a huge 'Télémaque,' with sprawling cuts," and of course a "De Sévigné." Supplying a hint of an equally voluminous correspondence, an unfinished letter was on a little writing-table, the files of papers belonging to which would have done honour to a

Secretary of State. A delicately enamelled gold snuff-box and a bag for knitting completed the picture.

The ladies saw a good deal of company, for Mrs. Murray Keith was fond of receptions and of patronage, and to both "husband" and "wife" their whist-table was indispensable.

In 1790, rendered anxious by a letter in which the Countess, their mother, referred to her increasing infirmities, Ladies Anne and Margaret came down on a six-weeks' visit to Scotland. Owing to some difficulty of accommodation, the sisters slept in the house of their sister-in-law, which was opposite to that of old Lady Bal, whom they were there to see. Lady Anne was comforted concerning her mother. The Countess was mellowed by age "as only strong wine mellows." Her anxieties for her family were set at rest. Her elder sons prospered. As for her soldier and sailor sons, they were bound to be content with winning the laurels which the spirited woman declared were, in her opinion, "very substantial food." Her son John was long ago released from his captivity.

His grievous privations, which, had his mother known of them earlier, must have cut her to the heart, were only the recollections of hardships which serve to point a soldier's tale, and make him welcome at every hospitable fireside. For William and James, who had died a sailor's and a soldier's death, they were but gone before, and, with their father, they would meet and welcome her in that haven to which her thoughts were more and more turning. Her temper had lulled and sweetened, if her memory was going from her. But while the past had to be recalled with difficulty, and by the help of others, the Countess could be brighter than she had ever been in the present. She was always more and more occupied with the future which the pages of her Bible promised her, "when we shall all be young together again, Annie," she said with pathetic yearning.

In compliment to her dear old mother, who frequently said, "Annie, I wish you would tell me how that unlucky business of Jeanie and Jamie ended," Lady Anne wrote her second part of "Auld Robin Gray." Though she sang it to her mother, she did not give even the Countess a copy of the sequel to the song. But motherly affection triumphed over failing nature, and the memory which could retain little else, preserved the fresh verses from Lady Anne's singing. Old Lady Balcarres was in the habit of repeating the second part of "Auld Robin Gray," with the pride of being the only person, beside her daughter Anne, who had the power of doing so. To Lady Anne's own account of the writing of the second part of "Auld Robin Gray," Mrs. Pringle, of Whytbank, added the following particulars:— "About that time a ballad entitled, 'A Continuation of Auld Robin Gray,' was sung in the streets, and published in magazines and newspapers, which greatly annoyed the family, and was very trying to the sweet temper of Lady Anne. But it was not considered worthy of being disclaimed. In order to prove its spurious origin, Lady Anne retired to her room, and in a short time produced the fragment from which Sir Walter Scott copied a verse in the 'Pirate.'" Mrs. Pringle, then much in George

Square, picked up the fragment from hearing Lady Balcarres reciting it. Mrs. Pringle did not get it in confidence, but she considered it in the light of a trust, and only put it on paper for one of Lady Anne's own early friends—Mrs. Russel, born a Rutherfurd, of Hyndford Place. On Mrs. Russel's death it is supposed that the copy fell into the hands of her sister, Miss Christy Rutherfurd, and from her passed to Sir Walter Scott—" the little nephew" of George Square. Sir Walter's confession confirms the explanation. He had heard the first part of "Auld Robin Gray" sung by his aunt, Mrs. Russel, and given by her without hesitation as the song of her old friend, Lady Anne Lindsay. Many years afterwards he had got seven or eight verses of the second part from Mrs. Russel's sister, another and very dear aunt, Miss Christy Rutherfurd, —the great friend of Mrs. Murray Keith. All these persons were perfectly convinced of her ladyship's right to the whole ballad, and the ballad's right to her ladyship.

On this visit to Edinburgh, Lady Anne found

her old friend, Mistress Cockburn, still alive, and wonderfully unaltered by age, while Soph Johnstone was rapidly shrivelling into a wretched miser.

Returned to London, Lady Anne and Lady Margaret would hail with keen curiosity and pitiful questioning the arrival in London, and the presentation at court, of the Countess of Albany, the widow of Charles Edward, the last of those Stuarts to whom the Lindsays had been blindly faithful. The sisters, in common with the mass of aristocratic England, were doomed to watch in wonder, sorrow, and horror, the events happening over in France,—from the fate of the king's soldiers at Versailles to the guillotining of Marie Antoinette,—and hastened to throw open their doors and hearts to the flocks of refugees with historic names—Richelieus, De Birons, De la Tremouilles. The mature women must have criticised sharply the new fashions—the caps, casques, tight skirts, shawls fastened on one shoulder, and the classic sandals, which were worn instead of the hats and feathers, the gowns with square-cut bodies, and bunchy trains pulled through the pocketholes, the red mantles, and the shoes with high heels which were in vogue when the Lindsays were girls. Surely the well-brought-up daughters of high-principled little Lady Bal raised their eyebrows, shrugged their shoulders, and turned their backs on the dances which were being introduced by Emma, Lady Hamilton. Sisters Anne and Margaret would crave once more, with bated breath, news of lost Lord Howe and his fleet. Was not their young brother Hugh, the cadet of the large family, in one of Howe's ships?

About this period Lady Anne, after having waited till she was upwards of forty years of age, married Andrew Barnard, Esq., son of the Bishop of Limerick, a handsome, pleasantly-gifted man, without much wealth, and somewhat her junior. It is said that Mr. Barnard was far from the first or the most distinguished pretender to Lady Anne's hand, but that beneath her gay ease and readiness there lurked a certain fickle indecision, as well as a certain contentment with the present, which was fatal to the hopes of the lovers. It is expressly told that she had kept her heart in her own possession till, in the afternoon of her life, she bestowed it on Mr. Barnard. That her choice in the end was to her perfect satisfaction every line which she wrote afterwards witnesses.

Misfortune continued to pursue Lady Margaret—"the most beautiful woman in Europe," as Lady Anne describes her. In Lady Margaret's prime, as in her promise, she wasted her affections. A second time she lavished them on a man "who sacrificed her life and happiness to his selfishness," not scrupling to extort the sacrifice while he refrained from fulfilling the obligation which would at least have given him a poor legal right to the womanly all of Lady Margaret's heart and fair prospects. Lady Anne had to part from her sister in these circumstances, to go with her husband to Ireland, where his father had the see of Limerick.

In 1797 Lady Anne accompanied Mr. Barnard to the Cape of Good Hope, whither he went as private secretary to Lord Macartney, when his lordship was appointed Governor of the new colony. The change from Berkeley Square to what was then the primitive Dutch Cape was a very plunge from high cultivation, with its excitements and diversions, to rude simplicity and bald nature. It was a test to Lady Anne's principles and temper. But she liked the change, and her principles and temper stood the test. In the absence of any lady of Lord Macartney's family, she enjoyed being what she called "the woman" of the station, and a very fair *Governess* she proved herself.

Lady Anne was a high-born lady, fresh from princely and noble society. The residents of Cape Town, duly impressed, looked up to her, while they could not help being flattered by her presidency over their society. She had a lively perception of the gulf which existed between the colonists and herself, and did not hesitate to let it be seen—always in the best-bred way. She could both keep her own place, and keep other people in theirs. But she was too good-humoured to be entirely supercilious. She did indulge (in her journal) in all sorts of droll observations on the ladies, characterising them as "mad in white muslin," with "no countenance, no manner, no graces;" but "with a vulgar smartness which told that the torch of Prometheus that animated them was made of mutton-tail." She conjectured that the dancing, "which was in a sort of pit-a-pat, tingling little step, and without halting a moment," had been learnt from some beauty on her way to Bengal; and she compared the unconscious self-satisfied dancers to such women as may be found in a country town "at an assize-ball a great way from the capital." She arrived at the characteristic conclusion that what these Dutch belles wanted most was "shoulders and softness of manners," and settled that she would thenceforth quite understand the term, " a Dutch doll."

But Lady Anne did more than take her fun out of the colonists. She really desired to recommend the English Government to the half-sullen conquered province. She had a feeling that it was her duty to keep the colonists in good-humour, and to improve, as far as possible, their tastes and habits by furnishing them with a fine example of English womanhood, ladyhood, and sovereignty. No woman could have been quicker in resources, or less guiltless of supposing that she could demean herself by any act of condescension, usefulness, or innocent amusement, as means to an end.

The next thing to admire in Lady Anne during her exile was her immense power of accepting a situation. Beyond praise are the zest and relish with which, after her confessed hearty appreciation of "the politest society," she turned to a traveller's compensations, and became again a child of nature as she had been in the farm-yard and the Den of Balcarres. She found treasures everywhere. The ignorance of her simple, buoyant intelligence was rather in her favour. She was neither bored nor bowed down by weighty authorities and scientific laws, and she did not harass herself with mental cramming before or after her excursions. To be told everything as she went along was her comfortable plan of gaining knowledge, of which her memory enabled her to appropriate and digest a surprising amount. Thus stories of families of rabbits every member blind of one eye, *king* bees whose sting was certain death, stones full of all colours of paint-powder, rose-trees blowing exactly at four o'clock each afternoon, were received with the utmost satisfaction, and swallowed almost without a struggle.

At the Castle, Lady Anne gave balls on the first day of every month, and tea and music every Thursday. She took the subaltern officers under her peculiar protection. At stated times she and Mr. Barnard entertained Lord Macartney, the aides-de-camp, or the town magnates to dinner; the burden of stimulating and supplementing the genius of Revel, the Swiss cook, falling upon Lady Anne. With a suspicion of her coming difficulties, she had carried with her from England " a map" of a quartered and subdivided ox and sheep for the instruction of the Dutch butchers. She insisted on an ample provision of light at her parties, using up for that purpose, on one occasion, the same wax-candles which had shone on the *élite* of London society, with a sprinkling of royal dukes, in Berkeley Square. Generally speaking, Lady

Anne managed all the etiquette, hospitality, and housekeeping of the Castle, and was a very busy and important woman.

She gave herself up to old and novel country pleasures when she and Mr. Barnard retired to their country-house of Paradise—a Dutch farm-house on the side of a mountain three thousand feet high, with rows of orange-trees in flower and fruit shading the windows. She fed her cats and chickens, she drew, she gardened.

Both, at the Castle and in Paradise, Lady Anne luxuriated in pets. She had a little tame buck that would fain have slept upon her feet. A couple of secretary-birds ("namesakes of Barnard's"), with long legs, black velvet breeches, and large wings, never ate standing, but sat down to dinner as regularly as did their master and mistress. A sea-calf was coaxed into living by having a teapot with milk thrust into his mouth every time he opened it to bleat. A penguin, resembling the old ladies who wore sacques with long ruffles, spent half its time in the pond with the calf, and half in the drawing-room with Lady Anne. Two jackals were the delight of the dogs, from their coquettishness; and two young wild cats were nursed by a dog. A horned owl was an emblem of wisdom, and a beautiful green chameleon, of folly.

Lady Anne was constantly over head and ears collecting specimens of Cape plants and animals —great rarities in those days—to take home with her or to send to her friends in England. She had the Lindsay affectionateness which kept her heart warm in absence, and enabled her to retain the kindly generosity of "sister Anne" of Balcarres. She was prone to serve others before herself, in true elder-sister fashion. Withal, it does sometimes strike us as if these acquisitions, and the enriching of her friends, formed a little too much the business of Lady Anne's life. From procuring a tiger-skin for the Prince Regent, and castor-oil seeds to mix with gold and other beads for the Queen and the Princesses, to endowing less exalted personages, she is never at rest in making her gains. Though she writes in good faith of her reluctance to ask for any curiosity which had

taken her fancy, and blames herself for false
delicacy and shyness, one does not remark the
presence of these qualities; and in spite of the
barter of good things which she effected, and
the invitations to the Castle which she freely dispensed to all who conferred favours on her, here
and there her progress reads like a spoiling
of the Egyptians. A doubt is left on the mind
whether Lady Anne did not share in the royal
and aristocratic delusion, that not only was
service to her its own reward, but that no claim
which she could proffer could be an exaction if
it was proffered for the sake of her friends. In
spite of this she was a humane, enlightened
woman, an agreeable secretary's wife, and deserved most of the simple enough spoil which
she did not scruple to take.

As Lady Anne had asked for the bit of oat-
cake from the butler at Balcarres from love
of variety, so she enjoyed every homely incident
of her life among the Dutch boors. It is enjoy-
able still to read the wonderfully lifelike ex-
tracts published from her journal. It is hardly
possible not to exalt "the blood and the breed-

ing," with their unflagging spirit. Her ascent of Table Mountain and her sleeping on it was a brilliant episode. Before starting, she had been guilty of a piece of waggery. "I had stolen a part of Barnard's wardrobe for precaution, which made him, as I bounded up the rocks, laugh, and call out, 'Heyday, Anne! what are these?' 'Yours, *meyne lieve vreunde*,' said I; 'you must acknowledge it is the first time you were ever conscious of my wearing them.'" The slave-guide smiled, and called her a "*braave vrow*,"—as Lady Anne translates it, "a rare wife,"—and she was very proud of the compliment. She left all the gentlemen behind her, "envying the *braave vrow*; her light heels being the effect, perhaps, of the lightness of her heart." She reached the top first. To find herself three thousand five hundred feet high, to behold a considerable town more invisible than the smallest miniature, and to feel the pure air invigorating her, "gave her a disembodied feeling." "And now," she said to her most learned companion, Mr. Barrow, with her habit of commanding, which was nevertheless a very bright habit in her, "thou man of infinite charts and maps, explain to me all that I see before me, and what I do not see. What is this? What is that? What are the different bays I hear you all wrangling about? And do not suppose that I am to clamber to the top of Table Mountain for nothing." Before giving each gentleman his bumper of Madeira to invigorate him for the descent, she made the request that all the party might unite in the full chorus of "God save the King," a request which was instantly complied with, "every hill—the Lion's Head, Lion's Rump, Devil's Hill, Hottentot Mountain—singing his part, as they (the company) had done before, till 'Great George' grew less at every turn, and at last gave up the ghost like a private gentleman in a valley." The lady and her squires had snipes for supper (on which she has the note: "N.B.—I believe we ate a dozen apiece at least"), the slaves lay round the fire, and "Barnard and I," so she wound up her narrative, "within our tent found a good bed, on which two heads reposed themselves that were truly grateful for all the blessings conferred on them, but most so for their happiness in each other."

A cluster of wandering stars rose on Lady Anne's horizon, in the shape of Lord Mornington, with his brother and suite, on his way to fill the Governor-generalship of India. These travellers brought with them a delightful waft of old associations, news from city and court. They were especially welcome to the "Governess" of the Cape of Good Hope. She had a natural sympathy with Governors-general, through her brother Balcarres, who was trying the office as Governor of Jersey before filling it on a greater scale as Governor of Jamaica, and several more of her brothers had been or were in India—where were not Lady Anne's brothers? But it was not to his Excellency that her ladyship awarded her hospitality first. She wrote, with true nobility of heart, that she and her husband would have been happy to accommodate people that they loved so much (a Governor-general, to boot), "had not the prior claims of the A——s as older friends, nearer friends, and *poorer friends*, made it impossible to sacrifice the holy motive to the agreeable attraction." Only the successful invasion of his enemies the bugs into his quarters brought the Governor-general as a humble petitioner for what the Barnards had not the heart to deny him—one of their back parlours.

The Barnards' tour into the interior, undertaken in the year of the Irish Rebellion, is an excellent specimen throughout of genteel comedy. The company, in addition to Lady Anne and Mr. Barnard, with their servants, included a young lady, the beauty of the colony, who was visiting Lady Anne, and Lady Anne's cousin Johnny, one of the innumerable Dalrymples—a cavalier of seventeen, who had been judiciously appointed aide-de-camp to the beauty on the journey. The beauty, it should be told, took every inconvenience *en route* as a personal injury.

The conveyance, sometimes drawn by horses, sometimes by bullocks, was a waggon, supplied with a wooden case to pack the travellers into. Each furnished his or her stock of necessaries. Mr. Barnard took the lead with the heavier *pièces de résistance*—hams, Hamburg beef, liqueurs, powder. The careful *haus-vrow* Anne Barnard followed. Besides "a conjuror" for cooking stews, pine-apple cheeses, a jar of Batavian ginger, tea, coffee, sugar, rice, and what her mother the Scotch countess would have called "the napery" of the expedition, she lugged with her a great assortment of coarse handkerchiefs, ribbons, beads, common knives, needles and thread, to dispense among the subjects of the Government. The beauty carried a selection from her wardrobe, and a knitting-case containing some pins, pen and ink, and a half-finished purse, dividing the care of the knitting-case between herself and her aide-de-camp.

For the convenience of shooting without loss of time any game which might start up, five loaded guns were slung in the waggon, and the only stipulation open to Lady Anne and the beauty was to have the guns placed where the ladies had the *least* chance of being shot.

On the front seat sat "the illustrious Gasper"

the driver, and behind him Lady Anne, on her knee the family drawing-book of the Barnards, which had descended from mitre to mitre, and found itself very much astonished at its present situation. By her sat the secretarius Barnard, for the express purpose of popping out at the partridges on half a minute's notice. Behind them again were Cousin Johnny and the beauty, seated on the woolsacks, viz., mattresses,. "a situation she said she preferred to the front seat, where she could have *only* seen the country. Johnny highly approved of her preferring this seat, as the country was not fit to be looked at." The common costume of the explorers—ladies and gentlemen alike—was great-coats.

Thus the cavalcade jogged across the sandy plains and skirted the table-lands in search of adventures. They rested every night at Dutch farm-houses, and partook, in so far as it was possible, of Dutch boors' fare—bock, fowls, pheasants, mutton-tail—paying or not paying for their entertainment as their compulsory hosts received or refused remuneration.. Lady Anne found every prosperous farmer's wife fatter than another, and with bigger monsters of children. So scornfully pitiful were these *booresses* of the Governess's childless state, that she got Mr. Barnard to consent to having four fictitious boys left in England. She would not have girls, lest people should say she neglected them; but she would leave four boys across the sea engaged in their education. Once, finding a childless matron like herself, she considerately suppressed her supposititious progeny, that she might not overwhelm her sister in misfortune.

The gentlemen found sport among the bocks and the pheasants. Johnny shot a pow, or wild peacock, which Lady Anne plucked for him, and they had it roasted and ate it as a great delicacy. Ladies and gentlemen visited a cave with petrifactions, where lions were *smelt* by the horses.

There was an overturn, out of which the beauty came "preserved, in the sweetest sense of the word, as the cask of ginger had had its top knocked off in the fall, and had poured its contents in at her neck and out at her toe, by which means she was a complete confection." On occasions the party dined off the top of a cask, and lay down to sleep like a company of strolling players. In an extreme case of a sluttish *ménage* the beauty wanted a clean cup, and the hostess presented her with a child's soiled nightcap to wipe the cup, out of which Mr. Prince (a clerk and auctioneer who attended on the secretary in the character of a courier) had just drunk. Unconquerable Lady Anne was so provoking as to hope this would have made the beauty laugh, but the poor beaten beauty was more ready to cry.

The travellers visited the Moravian missionaries, or Herrnhütters, and Lady Anne made them a gift of seeds. As the most gracious mark of her esteem, she presented them also with the flesh strawberry which had been sent to her by her sister Lady Margaret, "the most beautiful woman in Europe," believing that they were duly impressed by the last piece of information. Lady Anne was for ever drawing mountains and Hottentots. Everywhere she laid herself out to amass calabashes, serpents' skins, and Job's tears. Everywhere she lavished handkerchiefs, ribbons, and beads on the slaves as well as on their mistresses, on the Hottentots as well as on the Dutch, with now and then a bit of womanly thoughtfulness and partiality. Each boor was, will he nill he, hospitable; and as most of them declined payment in money, a large proportion of their fat wives got invitations to return Lady Anne's visit when they were down in Cape Town—an honour which she was surprised to see them take phlegmatically.

Mr. Barnard bought up a farm's whole stock of dried peaches, for which he had a liking; and he cured a boor of threatened gout in the stomach by administering timely glasses of Madeira. Lady Anne ordered a cargo of cured fish for winter use at the Castle, and longed to cut the tacked tongue of a dumb child, but did not dare to attempt it.

The family of the Van Rheimes stood out as quality among the boors. Van Rheime was a Cape Town man, disgusted with town life; his *vrow* was gentle and cleanly. His farm, with its underwood of aloes, was famous for its sport.

A hunting waggon, drawn by eight horses, in which Lady Anne and the beauty, not to be behind the gentlemen, accompanied their friends, galloped over the rough tracks within sight and aim of ostriches, pows, and bocks, while the crack and patter of the shooting went on without ceasing, on every side. There was fishing also to be had on the farm, and the Barnards' party, with the whole Van Rheime family, drove to the Breech Rivière, and saw the nets drawn. The produce was "a huge skate as large as a house, which sighed bitterly, and died with difficulty, and was ordered into oil." Over and above it were bécasse fish, similar to eels, but with bills like woodcocks. During another day's sport zebras were hailed at a distance.

The Barnards made their longest sojourn with the Van Rheimes. A regular friendship sprang up between the hosts and their guests. Mr. Barnard gave to Jacob Rheime a gun which the secretary had valued. Lady Anne gave to the *vrow* a little of everything that remained in her boxes, and, as a particular token of regard, she left her smelling-bottle, with its

double gold top. The heads and waists of
the children were tied up by Lady Anne's own
hands with scarlet and white ribbons. Every
slave was made happy with a handkerchief,
and scissors, thread, and needles, a knife, and
two schellings. Lady Anne records as a worthy
tribute to the memory of the Van Rheimes,
"Had I a fortnight at my command to spend
pleasantly, where I should be sure to be welcome, I should not make a scruple of going to
Jacob Van Rheime's, to partake of his fish from
his pond—the ocean, and of his bock from his
park of two hundred miles in circumference."

Lady Anne's journal reads very like an
earlier, rude cabinet version of Miss Eden's
"Up the Country." The Barnards' plan had
been to return from the Cape of Good Hope by
a circuitous route, including New South Wales,
Egypt, and Greece. To their regret, however,
the Peace of Amiens, in 1802, gave the colony
back to the Dutch. While Mr. Barnard was
obliged to remain at the Cape for a year to
settle colonial business, Lady Anne proceeded
to England with the fleet. Her purpose was to

endeavour to procure a situation under Government for her husband on his return; but her talents as well as her influence, in this respect, failed.

In England she found that women's hair had crept down to their eyebrows, and their waists up to their chins. Her friend the Prince Regent was not only married, as all his good subjects had wished him to be, to his cousin of Brunswick, but had come to grief in his character of husband. Lady Anne's connections, the Norths, were much mixed up with the impulsive, unruly, injured Princess of Wales. Lady Charlotte Lindsay, the Honourable John's wife, was one of the Princess's favourite ladies-in-waiting—altogether an awkward complication of relations for a friend of the Prince Regent's.

Miss Jeanie Rutherfurd's wonderful little nephew had brought out the "Minstrelsy of the Border"—a work after Lady Anne's heart. He was just about to publish "Marmion." Jane Austen and Maria Edgeworth were writing their novels of real life; Mrs. Radcliffe her romances; and Elizabeth Hamilton her popular tale of the "Cottagers of Glenburnie;" while Joanna Baillie was putting on the stage (the worst place where they could have been put) her "Plays of the Passions." Mary Berry had become the intimate friend of Elizabeth, Countess of Hardwicke, by the instrumentality of Joanna's brother, Dr. Baillie, and, through Mary Berry, Lady Anne ought to have known Joanna Baillie. But Joanna was no fine lady, nor was she a woman of fashion. Distinguished woman of letters as she was, she led a simple retired life with her mother and sister at Hampstead, while Lady Anne did not quit her own sphere, not even to meet Sir Walter when, in the zenith of his fame, he went up, once and again, to London, to be *fêted* and lionised.

Lady Anne travelled down to Scotland in 1803—4 to see her mother. The Countess and her "husband," Mrs. Keith, had returned to end their days at Balcarres. Earl Alexander, though he had found an honourable escape from his main difficulties by his governorships, had been forced to give up Balcarres, and retain his wife's estate of Haigh Hall. However, the *château* and its farms were not doomed to pass from the Lindsays. The Honourable Robert redeemed them, reserving to his brother the right of repurchase, which Earl Alexander did not choose to exercise. It was with Robert Lindsay and his wife and family that the two attached old ladies had taken up their residence. Lady Anne, after her exile, enjoyed revisiting "the dear old nest," where, as she said, "eleven brother and sister chickens had been hatched and fostered, who through life had never known once what it was to peck at each other." It is very likely that on this and on future visits Lady Anne was lodged in the room termed "Cromwell's room," from its repute of having been slept in by the Protector: it was on the same stair, but lower down than her less dignified perch of earlier days.

Before Lady Anne saw Balcarres again, a cloud of misfortune had darkened over her, such as that which the Lindsays had encountered in 1780—4, when Captain James was killed, and Captain John was in the hands of Hyder Ali. She had returned to England in time for the great sight of Nelson's funeral, and for the public lamentation over the death of William Pitt; but private losses were about to sweep all others out of her mind. In 1808 she sustained a heavy blow in the death of her husband, after a true union of fourteen or fifteen years.

Mr. Barnard had requested in his will that Lady Anne would send testimonies of his regard to those friends whom she knew he honoured and esteemed. She had engravings taken from his picture, and sent one to the Prince Regent. His Royal Highness, whose own matrimonial experience had been disastrous, was sufficiently moved to write a note expressive of his gratitude, condolence, and, above all, remembrance of old times.

In the same year Lady Anne's nephew, the Earl of Hardwicke's eldest son and heir, Lord Royston, perished by the wreck of his yacht during a storm in the Baltic. He was a fine young man of twenty-four, with all the Lindsays' love of letters, and he was so ardent a traveller that he had been absent from England since before the attainment of his majority.

In June of the following year Miss Berry mentions being at an assembly at Lady Margaret Fordyce's, where were present the Princess of Wales, with her lady-in-waiting, Lady Charlotte Lindsay, and Lady Charlotte's sister, Lady Glenburnie. There is no mention of Lady Anne Barnard as having been there. Possibly she did not go out in those days, or she stood out against identifying herself with the Princess, continuing reluctant to believe that the "finest gentleman" was the worst husband in Europe. Later in the same year, 1809, Lady Anne and Lady Margaret once more went together to Scotland and Balcarres. This seems to have been Lady Margaret's (if not Lady Anne's) last return home. Lady Anne describes the time as saddened by the sense that the heart which would have rejoiced with theirs was still, and by the inevitable contrast between this and former sojourns. The sisters found their mother without a complaint, though she was now eighty-two. She was oppressed only by the want of memory, "which being known and acknowledged, gave her no concern." The old Countess was handed down to dinner every day by her youngest grandson, aged five years. There were only seventy-seven years between the cavalier and his lady, "who did not feel quite happy unless she had a few compliments paid to her on her dress and good looks."

Lady Anne and Lady Margaret remained over the great family festival, that was at once their mother's birthday and Christmas Day. Each member of the family presented the venerable heroine of the occasion with his or her *cadeau*, and Lady Anne put hers, a black lace cloak, over "the nice little figure," and wished her mother many happy returns of the day. "She seemed proud and pleased—her eyes sparkled with unusual intelligence. 'Is not this too fine for me?' she said; 'but I accept it with pleasure, and in return, Annie, I will make you a present which I hope you will live to enjoy the benefit of. I mean the knowledge that old age is not the miserable state that people suppose it to be; on the contrary, it is one of calm enjoyment. . . . . . The thoughts of that untried country, Annie, to which I am invited by my Saviour, are to me the source of inexhaustible delight. I trust,' said she with fervour, 'that I shall there meet with you all again, through His merits, in perpetual youth and endless happiness. And this castle of mine, Annie, is not a *château d'Espagne*, as Madame Annie Keith calls some of my projects when she does not approve of them.'"

In 1810 Lady Anne still had her house at Wimbledon. The poor Hardwickes removed to it to be out of the way of receiving people, after Dr. Baillie had gone down to Wimpole Hall only to see the last of "little Charlie," their second and sole surviving son.

Shortly afterwards Lady Anne must have taken up house again with Lady Margaret in their old quarters of Berkeley Square. But "changes were the order of the day," and this reunion was to be of brief duration. Lady Margaret's disloyal and cruel lover had goaded, by slow torture, a spirit meek as that of a saint, so that she turned upon him at last.

While "his conduct latterly inspired her with

the disdain it merited," a deep resentment utterly foreign to Lady Margaret's character corroded her heart. Lady Anne witnessed the work with indignation and pain. She declared that it was only "at the earnest instance of affection," and "upon a solemn occasion of religious duty," that she prevailed on her sister to abjure for ever a sentiment contrary to the spirit of Christian forgiveness of injuries. "She did so when taking the sacrament in Dublin" (it might be from the hand of the gentle Charles Lindsay, the likest to Lady Margaret of any member of the family), and peace was restored to her mind. But it was too late for youth, beauty, and health, which had all fled.

Yet the clinging heart could not continue to beat without a new stay round which it might wind its tendrils. At an advanced period of life Lady Margaret became the third wife of a worthy and cultivated gentleman, "who, as he then acknowledged, had been attached to her almost from infancy," notwithstanding that he had twice married in the interval. This Jacob was Sir James Bland Burgess, an old pupil of Dr. Somerville's. Sir James was member for Helstone, Secretary of State for Foreign Affairs, and Knight-Marshal of the Household. He was literary, like the rest of these literary people, with whom the malady seemed not merely hereditary, but infectious. He was the author of "The Birth and Triumph of Love," and "Richard I.," an epic poem, scarcely so well known as the household song of "Auld Robin Gray." He had married first Elizabeth Noel, daughter of Viscount Wentworth; then Anne, daughter of Lieutenant-Colonel Montolieu; and at last he married his first love, Lady Margaret Fordyce.

Lady Margaret's marriage took place in the year 1812—the great year when London was again and again illuminated for Lord Wellington's Peninsular victories. Lady Anne must have recalled how Lord Mornington, when she was his hostess and "Governess" of the Cape of Good Hope, had talked to her, and afterwards written to her, of his brother Arthur's exploits in India. This was the season, too, when Lady Hardwicke gave her famous private theatricals, her friends being tormented by hundreds of hopeless applications for tickets. When the audience was graced by the presence of the Prince Regent and two royal dukes, not to speak of the two banished French Dukes of Berri and Bourbon, what green-room could have been better fitted with an ally and assistant, if Lady Anne, as she surely did, looked in behind the scenes?

Lady Margaret Burgess was comforted by the consideration and kindness of her second husband, and by the regard of his children, to whom she proved a mild stepmother. She was happier than her friends had ever known her; but she was worn out and weary in the midst of her happiness, and she died, in devout readiness to obey her Master's call for her to depart, within two years of her marriage.

Lady Margaret's last illness and death occurred in the most brilliant year of the decade, '14. On the arrival in England of the allied princes, Mary Berry, in her journal, makes constant reference to her association with Lady Hardwicke and Lady Charlotte Lindsay; but the name of Lady Anne Barnard—not the least distinguished of the four—never once occurs, an absence which may be accounted for by the circumstance of what was to Lady Anne a special bereavement.

Though Lady Anne was far from withdrawing from the society of her kindred and friends during the next ten years, she seems to have lived less in the world after the deaths of her husband and sister. What she said with regard to her contribution to the family memoirs, she might have said of the late autumn of her life, which had boasted its own time of picturesque incident and interest: "Having for the present closed all that it is necessary to say of kings and courts, I return to the haunts of my heart, like the traveller who has been long away, gleaning from other countries what may amuse the dear circle at home, grieving with tenderness over chasms in that circle—never to be filled up; but grateful for what remains of friendship and affection still on earth to cheer the evening of life."

Lady Anne added, on her own account, "Of

Elizabeth's (Lady Hardwicke's) society I have all that I can in reason expect from the avocations which, as a mother and a grandmother to four families, multiply themselves upon her every day. My brothers rally round me with kindness when business calls them to town; but it is in the affection of my two nephews (Lord Lindsay and my young guardsman, James, son of Robert Lindsay) I find the tenderness so unusual in young men, which is ever ready to fly to be my prop and support when I feel a want of it. No ostentation is to be found in their attentions. They do not tease me with solicitudes about my health, with giving me chairs when I do not wish to sit down, or asking me to drink wine, or to be helped to what at home I may venture to ask for. All is liberty and equality here, untaxed by restraint; it is granted by them to me, and by me to them; even their wives permit me to steal into my own den (my drawing-room, of forty feet long, surrounded with papers and drawings), and employ myself all the morning without thinking themselves ill-used by my absence. . . . . My friends press me to go out to amuse myself; but I should go without any interest beyond the charm of getting home again. By the side of my fire I have got into the habit of living in other days with those I loved, reflecting on the past, hoping in the future, and sometimes looking back with a sorrowful retrospect where I fear I may have erred. Together with those mental employments I have various sources of improvement. I compile and arrange my memorandums of past observations and events; I retouch some sketches, and form new ones from souvenirs taken on the spot. Sometimes I employ an artist to finish these, but all is first traced accurately with my own pencil, so impossible do I find it to get any one to enter exactly into the spirit of my subject. With such entertainment for my mornings, and a house full of nephews and nieces, together with the near connections of my dear Barnard, all tenderly attached to me, I have great, great reason to bless God, who, in taking much from me, has left me so much."

One of these nephews, when asked by a younger member of his house to give some account of Lady Anne as she was at this time, declared that it would be no easy matter to draw the portrait of one whose charms and weaknesses were so intermingled. He dwelt on her benevolence and her power of giving and receiving pleasure. He had often seen her change a disagreeable party into an agreeable one; she could make the dullest speak, the shyest feel happy, and the witty flash fire, without any apparent exertion. He loved her as a mother, and so did all who dwelt under her roof. He gave a characteristic anecdote of her. "She was entertaining a large party of distinguished guests at dinner, when a hitch occurred in the kitchen. The old servant came up behind her, and whispered, 'My lady, you must tell another story; the second course won't be ready for five minutes.'" Is there not an anecdote almost the same told of Madame Maintenon?

Of the sprightliness which won for the Lindsays the distinctive term "light Lindsays,"—the lightness, contrary to a common acceptation of the word, being often rooted in honest, unquestioning piety,—Lady Anne had her full share. It continued with her almost unabated, as did the pleasant self-satisfaction of her easy autocratical tone, her frank and genial affability. We rarely have such unstinted, unbroken sprightliness in women now.

We may no longer hope to meet with such genuine gaiety of heart as electrified the listless aides-de-camp and subalterns, and even, by help of an interpreter, delighted the stolid Dutch boors and their fat wives, when Lady Anne was Governess of the Cape, the indomitable spirit within her finding ample fund for quips and flights when she was a widow well up in years. Our self-satisfaction has been rudely shaken; the most autocratical of us has been lifted bodily from her pedestal. As a rule a higher goal of good causes men and women more frequently to fall in the race, and to halt painfully after the falling. "Deeper and more elevated feelings, where they exist to any appreciable extent, must cast at least some shadow over the soul that possesses them." That shadow, intensifying and softening human nature, will, on the other hand, take from its limpid, shallow brightness.

But while we would not recall the lower standard, the surface sparkle of good-humour which prevailed among our grandmothers, and while we are willing to pay the full penalty for something better, we are fain to look back wistfully on that constant blitheness which we have in a measure lost, and to acknowledge heartily all that was true and sweet in its origin.

Countess Anne still survived at Balcarres in great old age, "happy with her knotting," and "entranced with her Bible and the lives of the patriarchs."

In 1815 the battle of Waterloo shook, like a thunder-peal, the quiet homes of age, especially homes like that of the Lindsays, where the nephews and grandsons of a noble race of soldiers had in course of years taken their fathers' places in the field. At Tunbridge, Lady Hardwicke was one of the four ladies who held each a plate at church after a sermon in aid of a collection for the wounded at Waterloo.

In literature, Walter Scott and Byron had taken the place of Cowper and Darwin. Edmund Kean and Miss O'Neill were playing on the London boards, in the room of Elliston, John Kemble, and Mrs. Siddons.

In 1816 Lady Anne for a time lost the society of her sister Hardwicke by the marriage of her daughter, Lady Elizabeth Yorke, to Sir Charles Stuart, afterwards Lord Stuart de Rothesay, English Ambassador in Paris. Lord and Lady Hardwicke and Miss Berry accompanied the couple to Paris, which had become a kind of *terra incognita* to the English since the old days of Horace Walpole's friendship with Madame Dudevant. The party inspected the scenes — having still a horrible freshness to strangers—of the French Revolution, attended the court of the restored Bourbons, and visited the remnant of the old noblesse in the Faubourg St. Germain. Lady Anne could watch their progress from her arm-chair, and hear their adventures, altogether different from those of her waggon tour in Africa, with sympathy as entire as that which she had given to the domestic joys and sorrows of the "little Elizabeth" of Balcarres, whom Lady Anne lived to see the mother of the four peeresses of Mexborough, Caledon, Somers, and Stuart de Rothesay.

Lady Anne was kept informed of the old Countess's secure and perfect contentment, and did not fail on her part in affectionate and dutiful attention. But no trace occurs of Lady Anne's having gone down again to visit her mother at Balcarres. In 1816 Countess Anne entered her ninetieth year, and a letter was written to Lady Anne giving all the little family details of the long celebrated birthday. How the Countess's health was drunk by a numerous party, and the door was left open between the dining-room and bedroom, that she might hear the cheers with which it was received. In return, she drank a bumper to the health of her descendants, old friends, and neighbours, and sent back to them a feeble cheer. In the drawing-room her own gift of a hundred-guinea vase to her daughter-in-law was displayed, to the Countess's great satisfaction. And in the very hour of enjoyment Lady Anne's remembrance of the day had presented itself, and her mother insisted on having the two pretty boxes her daughter Anne had sent her in her own keeping.

In 1817 Lady Hardwicke was able to be down in Scotland, and to bring back to Lady Anne a personal report of their mother.

In 1818 a tie dating three-quarters of a century back was dissolved by the death at Balcarres of Mrs. Anne Murray Keith; but the Countess was far beyond human grief. In forgetting everything she never quite forgot this loss, very temporary as she felt it; yet she only remembered it to have much pleasure in hearing the circumstances of her friend's last moments repeated to her, calling the narrative "a bonnie story, and very edifying," and forbidding her attendants to regret Mrs. Keith's death any more than Lady Margaret's, or that of any other true Christian "who escaped easily and beautifully from the world."

In 1820 Lady Anne wrote to the Countess a touching letter from a daughter of seventy to a mother of ninety-three.

"My dearest Mother,

"I received your sweet message by James Lindsay, desiring me to pray for you sometimes. Sure I am that I ought to ask you to do the same for me, as I have little doubt of your possessing a better interest in the heavenly mansions than your poor Annie, whose views, alas! are not yet so much detached from this world as yours are; but I hope they will follow your example, and that we shall meet again as blessed spirits after we are purified from the foibles that flesh is heir to. Meantime you must on your part do something for me. Allow the painter I send you from Edinburgh, who is an intelligent man, to take your picture exactly as you are. You will be more valuable to us sitting cheerfully, composedly, and apparently far advanced in life as we all hope to be, in your chair, than if he was to make a young Venus of you. God bless my dear mother, and give her as many healthy and happy years as she can desire to enjoy before 'the renovation of youth and nature' arrives, which old Lord Mansfield told me, not long before his death, he was then expecting with patient hope.

"Ever and ever,
"Your affectionate and dutiful daughter,
"ANNE BARNARD."

The painter went and executed his commission, and the ancient lady, done with the business of life, was "infinitely pleased and gratified," instead of plagued by the ordeal.

In answer to this letter of Lady Anne's, her mother sent her the message, "Tell Annie that

'My wheel I turn round, but I come little speed,
For my hand is grown feeble, and weak is my thread;'"

quoting from the second part of "Auld Robin Gray," of which the Countess had been chosen to be the sole keeper, and all the verses of which she could repeat almost to her last day. She could still find occupation in her work and delight in her Bible. In summer she enjoyed her garden-chair, which took her sometimes as far as the turnip-fields which Earl James had been so eager about a long lifetime before. She was treated with such tender delicacy by her good son and his wife that she came to believe Balcarres was her own again, and the two, with their family, were her guests; so that it was a pretty and a proper piece of respect which they paid to their hostess and the lady of the house, as well as their mother, that they should come and sit with her for half an hour and read her a chapter or a hymn every evening before she retired to rest.

But the flame of life was very low in the socket, and in the year 1820, Countess Anne, then in her ninety-fourth year, died an almost painless death, and was laid to rest with the chivalrous old husband of her youth, and with the cousin and friend whom she had named in merry mockery the husband of her age,—Mrs. Murray Keith having bequeathed her body as a fitting legacy to the ivied chapel of Balcarres.

Lady Anne survived her mother nearly five years. In the same year with Countess Anne died her "old flirt"—as she used to call him, alluding to his courteous attentions to her— King George III.; and with the hasty return to England of the Princess of Wales in order to procure her coronation, followed the impeachment and trial of Queen Caroline. Lord Hardwicke was on the committee in the Lords. Lady Charlotte Lindsay having been for a period of years a lady-in-waiting, and a favourite with the Queen, underwent a searching and lengthened public examination. Lady Charlotte's honest, impartial evidence, which in the main was in the Queen's favour, received deserved praise; but when they questioned her on family misfortunes, and referred to the deaths of her brother Francis and her sister Lady Glenburnie, which had happened within a few weeks of each other, she burst into tears. Dr. Lushington, one of Queen Caroline's counsel, in commenting upon Lady Charlotte's evidence, by implication brought a charge against her husband which not only made Lady Charlotte feel deeply aggrieved, but must have caused a pang of indignant pain to Lady Anne, and to every member of the united and loyal Lindsays. Dr. Lushington suggested broadly that Colonel the Honourable John Lindsay, living in a little island near Guernsey, apart from his wife, on account of the state of his affairs, had sold to the Government party the letters which his wife had written to him on his being proposed for the office of chamberlain in the Princess of Wales's household. Far better that John Lindsay should have died a soldier's honourable death with his brother James, or that he should have perished in his captivity at Seringapatam, than that such an accusation had been established.

But Lord Balcarres, in his remonstrance in the House of Lords against the insulting inference which would have fatally compromised his brother, reminded Dr. Lushington conclusively that the letters which the Honourable John Lindsay was supposed to have sold, were those of the very woman whose personal influence over him prevented his accepting the office of chamberlain. Dr. Lushington withdrew his half statement with a sufficient apology.

It does not appear that he had any authority whatever for his suggestion, beyond the thoughtlessness and rashness which John Lindsay, in the following explanation, admitted: "About four years before this trial, the Princess of Wales had been anxious to appoint him her chamberlain, with a salary of four hundred pounds per annum, upon condition that he and Lady Charlotte should reside with her in the palace of Rastadt, where she at that time intended to live. Lady Charlotte then explained to her husband the reasons why she did not wish the proposal to be accepted. Colonel Bayley was at this time the Governor of Guernsey; Colonel Lindsay lived alone, and was frequently visited by Colonel Bayley. The consequence of this intimacy was that Colonel Lindsay very imprudently confided to him all that had passed between him and his wife on the subject of this appointment, and occasionally read him passages from her letters. Colonel Bayley was a confidential friend at Carlton House, and these communications were passed on and received there with avidity. Colonel Lindsay had no idea he was communicating with an agent of the King's, until an offer was made to him of any number of soldiers that he might require to work his stone quarries, and of various other conveniences of which he was in need, upon condition that he should give up the letters. This he refused to do, and it opened his eyes at once to the imprudence he had committed."

In 1821, died Napoleon Bonaparte, who had been the scourge and terror of Europe for the better part of Lady Anne's life, on that little islet rock off which her young brother William had been drowned.

Only the year before her death Lady Anne was confessing the spells of the Wizard of the North, although oddly enough she had failed to recognise either in Mr. Scott the poet, or in the Author of "Waverley," the little lame prodigy of her early friend and his aunt, Miss Jeanie Rutherfurd.

When reading the "Pirate," Lady Anne came upon a verse from the second part of her "Auld Robin Gray." High praise was awarded to the ballad, and it was assigned to Lady Anne Barnard.

Careless as Lady Anne was of literary reputation, she could not but derive satisfaction from appreciation so honourable and so unexpected. Added to the gratification was the pretty puzzle of where the Author of "Waverley" could have read or heard the second part of "Auld Robin Gray," when she had not made a single friend proud by the possession of a copy.

Lady Anne wrote to Sir Walter, with the arch request "that you will convey to the Author of 'Waverley,' with whom I am informed you are personally acquainted, how gratefully I feel the kindness with which he has (in the second volume of the 'Pirate,' thirteenth chapter) so distinguishedly noticed, and by his powerful authority assigned, the long-contested ballad of 'Auld Robin Gray' to its real author."

She confessed that the position in which she had placed herself with regard to the song, had at last become irksome to her. She asked how she could so fully mark her thankfulness to him who had relieved her from her dilemma, as by transmitting to him (more than half a century after the incident had happened) fairly and frankly the origin, birth, life, death, and confession, will and testament of "Auld Robin

Gray," with the assurance that the Author of "Waverley" was the first person out of her own family who had ever had any explanation from her on the subject. She then entered into the details of the composition of both parts of the ballad, and announced her conjecture that it was through Mrs. Murray Keith, her own and her mother's friend, and his friend also, that several verses of the second part had reached the Author of "Waverley." Lady Anne referred to the existence of another version of the second part from Jeanie's own lips, but promised that "that which has been already so highly honoured as to be placed where it is, shall for ever keep its ground with me, and the other shall remain in the corner of my portfolio." The end of the letter is characteristic :—

"Let me now once more, my dear sir, entreat that you will prevail on the Author of 'Waverley' to accept, in testimony of my most grateful thanks, of the only copies of this ballad ever given under the hand of the writer; and will *you* call here, I pray, when you come next to

London, sending up your name that you may
not be denied. You will then find the doors
open wide to receive you, and two people will
shake hands who are unacquainted with *ennui*
—the one being innocently occupied from
morning to night, the other with a splendid
genius as his companion wherever he goes.
"God bless you!
"ANNE BARNARD."

Sir Walter responded readily to this letter:
gave an account of his antecedents where the
song was concerned, and identified himself with
Lady Anne's youthful days and recollections.
Afterwards Lady Anne wrote to him, as he told
Basil Hall, one of the kindest letters he had
ever received, and a good deal of agreeable
correspondence passed between them. One
result of it was the printing and circulating by
Sir Walter, with Lady Anne's permission, of
"Auld Robin Gray," in a thin quarto volume,
among the members of the Bannatyne Club of
1824. But the meeting which Lady Anne had
desired never took place.

Lady Anne found occupation to the end—she was so enamoured of occupation that she had a paper expressly recommending it—among what she called her vagrant scraps. In it she wrote, "When alone, I am not above five-and-twenty. I can entertain myself with a succession of inventions, which would be more effective if they were fewer. I forget that I am sixty-eight, and if by chance I see myself in the glass looking very abominable—I do not care. What is the moral of this? That as far as my poor experience goes (and it is said that we must all be fools or physicians at forty), occupation is the best nostrum in the great laboratory of human life for pains, cares, mortifications, and *ennui*."

Lady Anne had written other verses besides "Auld Robin Gray;" "Where tarries my Love?" doubtless, among them. It is said that at Sir Walter Scott's request she made a collection of these, and of similar verses by other members of her family, and had gone so far as to prepare for the press a volume, entitled, "Lays of the Lindsays." But the halting indecision which formed part of her character, and perhaps a little scorn for intellectual influence, in women—apart from the *rôle* of *dame de société*, which she had played well in her day — interfered, and the volume was suppressed.

As illustrative of this scornful phase in Lady Anne's character, one remembers the words, half jesting as they were, "with which," in the sentence of a descendant, "the authoress closed an impertinent cross-examination to which the secretary of some antiquarian society, deputed to inquire into the matter, had subjected her." (She herself described the interview in a better spirit to Sir Walter Scott, explaining that Mr. J—— had endeavoured to entrap the truth from her in a manner which she had resented; but had he asked the question obligingly, she would have told him the fact distinctly but confidentially.) Her words were:—"The ballad in question has in my opinion met with attention beyond its deserts. It set off with having a very fine tune put to it by a doctor of music; was sung by youth and beauty for five years and more; had a romance composed from it by a man of eminence; was the subject of a play, of an opera, of a pantomime; was sung by the united armies in America, acted by Punch, and afterwards danced by dogs in the street—*but never more honoured than by the present investigation.*"

The task which Lady Anne had finally set herself was to sort the family papers for family perusal—to carry them forward by her own recollections, and by procuring from her brothers narratives and anecdotes of their experiences.

How many suns had set, and on what different coasts, since the child Lady Anne stood on tip-toe in her blue and yellow brocade, with round eyes and mouth, and defied frost-nips to fingers and toes, while she inspected curiously the unpacking of the red-nosed Laird of Macfarlane's contribution of the store in the plaiden bundle, which was carefully deposited in Earl James's closet a little later! The girl sympathised half ignorantly in the eagerness with which her father forgot asthma and gout, in order to turn over the musty packets, every now and then clutching and gloating on a treasure.

"It was a sweet satisfaction" to Lady Anne, her brother Lord Balcarres observed, that as she advanced in years, she not only realised the enjoyment of life in a delightful amusement, but had also the gratifying and conscious pleasure that she was obeying the earnest wish of her honoured father, who, knowing her ability, had urged her to continue a family record of which he had set an example.

Lady Anne's own statement was :—"I took up my pen and wrote—at first with a little pain. To turn back in fancy to the season of rose-buds and myrtles, and to find one's self travelling on in reality to that of snow-drops and cypresses, is a position which may naturally produce some inequality of style—the more so as I was often tempted by the gaiety and truthfulness of my old journals to transcribe from them *verbatim*, while on other occasions I have allowed the prudent and concise pen of the old lady to lop and abridge in a manner that I fear has greatly injured the spirit and originality of the work, though it has brought it into a more reasonable compass."

Lady Anne's task was highly congenial to her. She had in full what she termed "the family taste of spinning from the brain in the sanctum of the closet." She was persuaded of the truth of old Earl James's dogma, that "as every man has felt, thought, invented, or observed, a little of that genius which we receive from nature, or a little of that experience which we buy in our walk through life, if bequeathed to the community, would ultimately become a collection to do honour to the family where such records are preserved." No papers on earth could have had to her a tithe of the interest implied in the papers of the family in the honour and prosperity of which she was "built up." Her "serene, placid, and contented old age" was not rendered melancholy by pondering on the days that were no more. Lady Anne cherished a bright conviction of lasting re-union with the family she had loved so well. Thus dwelling on old stories, and surrounded in fancy by dear old faces in the dear old home, death, not unwelcome, found her.

Lady Anne Barnard died in 1825, in the house in Berkeley Square so long occupied by Lady Anne and Lady Margaret, and shortly after the death of her brother, Earl Alexander, at Haigh Hall, Lancashire. Lady Anne's brother, Charles, Bishop of Kildare, and her sister, Elizabeth, Countess of Hardwicke,* with the longevity of not a few of their predecessors, survived—the last of Lady Anne's generation—till far down in the present century.

In her prose composition Lady Anne's style reaches that degree of excellence when one ceases to think of style. It is always natural and graphic. As a family biographer, while she is sensible, candid, tender, and witty, she is not quite free from the usual faults of family biographers, verbiage and partiality. But, unquestionably, as her recollections were written for the family circle, they are entitled

* Said to have been the last survivor of the children painted by Sir Joshua Reynolds.

to more allowance on these points. The inequality of style, which she herself detected, peeps out, and the expression of her thoughts is more apt to be rambling and disjointed than when they were laid before the reader with the vivid simplicity and humour of her Cape Journal.

"Auld Robin Gray" was one of those happy hits of genius, by which at a stroke, almost without trouble and in unconsciousness, a result is produced which no amount of labour could add to or improve. Wherever Scotchmen dwell, wherever the Scotch language is understood, even by those who are not Scotch by birth and belongings, "Auld Robin Gray" is prized as being what Sir Walter Scott called it, "a real pastoral, which is worth all the dialogues Corydon and Phillis have had together from the days of Theocrites downwards." Versions of "Auld Robin Gray" are almost as numerous and various as its admirers, but Sir Walter Scott and Lord Lindsay have preserved the original. Modern taste frequently omits the first verse, fitting introduction to the story though it is :—

"When the sheep are in the fauld, when the kye's a' at hame,
And a' the weary warld to rest are gane,
The woes o' my heart fa' in showers frae my e'e,
Unkent by my gudeman, wha sleeps sound by me."

With 'regard to the incident—"To mak the crown a pound," Lady Anne informed Sir Walter Scott that the old Laird of Dalzell gave her a lawyer's advice, the antiquarian acumen of which delighted her. "My dear," he said to her in *tête-à-tête*, "the next time you sing that song alter the line about the crown and the pound; and when you have said that 'saving a crown' Jamie 'had naething else beside,' be sure that you add 'to mak it twenty marks my Jamie gaed to sea,'— for a Scotch pund, my dear, is but twenty pence, and Jamie wasna siccan a gowk as to leave Jeanie and gang to sea to lessen his gear. 'Twas that sentence," he whispered, "telled me the song was written by some bonnie lassie that didna ken the nature o' the Scotch money as well as an auld writer in the town o' Edinbro' would hae done."

Sir Walter's commentary on the advice is equally good. "I think Dalzell's criticism rather hypercritical, but very characteristic. . . . A crown, I would say, is no denomination of Scotch money, and therefore the pound to which it is to be augmented is not a Scotch pound. If it were objected to my exposition that it is unnatural that Jamie should speak of any other denomination of coin than the Scotch, I would produce you a dozen of old papers to prove that the coast of Fife in ancient times carried on a great trade with Holland and other countries, and of course French crowns and pounds sterling were current denominations among them. Moreover, he shows himself so ready to gang to sea, that, for aught I can tell, or Dalzell either (if he were alive), Jamie may have gone a trial voyage already, and speaks rather as a mariner than in the usual style of 'poor Scotland's gear.'"

In the line—

"His ship was a wrack—why didna Jamie dee?"

the name is commonly tampered with, and not, as Sir Walter Scott thought, to the improvement of the original. "I observe an alteration in 'Auld Robin' in an important passage," he remonstrated, referring to the copy which Lady Anne herself had sent him.

"'His ship was a wrack—why didna Jeanie dee?'

I have usually heard or read it 'Why didna Jamie dee?' I am not quite sure whether in their mutual distress the wish that Jamie had not survived, beloved as he was, is not more deeply pathetic than that which she utters for her own death. Besides, Jamie's death is immediately connected with the shipwreck, and her own more remotely so."

"Your query," replied Lady Anne, "is a very natural one. When I wrote it first it was 'Why didna Jamie dee?' Would he not have been happier dead than seeing my wretchedness and feeling his own? But the pens of others have changed this to their own fancy. . . . I feel the justness of your criticism, and from the first meant it to be as you recommend it."

The wistfulness of "auld Robin's" petition,

"Jeanie, for their sakes, will ye *no* marry me?"

is decidedly marred by the ordinary omission, small as it is, of the "no."

The two verses which contain the woefully summed-up tragedy have sustained transformation and mutilation :

"My father urged me sair—my mother didna speak,
But she looket in my face till my heart was like to break ;
They gied him my hand—my heart was *in* [not *at*] the sea—
And so Robin Gray he was gudeman to me.

"I hadna been his wife a week but only four,"

"When" (not "sitting so mournfully at a neighbour's door,") but

"mournfu' as I sat on the stane at my door,
I saw my Jamie's ghaist, for I couldna think it he,
Till he said, 'I'm come hame, love, to marry thee.'"

Whoever has seen the primitive seat, common in the locality of the song, will witness to the superiority of the first version.

The next verse has suffered much ; it is generally rendered—

"Oh, sair did we greet, and mickle did we say,
We took but ae kiss and tore oursel's away ;

VOL. II.   H

> I wish that I were dead, but I'm no like to dee,
> And auld Robin Gray is gudeman to me."

Lady Anne wrote it with more telling touches:—

> "Oh! sair, sair did we greet, and mickle say o' a',
> I gi'ed him ae kiss and bade him gang awa';
> I wish that I were dead, but I'm no like to dee,
> For tho' my heart is broken, I'm young, woe's me!"

There can be no doubt that the song ends fitly with the verse—

> "I gang like a ghaist, and I carena to spin,
> I darena think on Jamie, for that would be a sin;
> But I'll do my best a gude wife to be,
> For oh! Robin Gray he is kind to me."

Though it may sound paradoxical, the completeness of the song as a work of art lies not only in the fatal chain of circumstances to which the innocent lovers are victims, but in their faithful submission to inevitable misfortune, and the struggle after duty, which is sure to be triumphant in the end, though it be a thorn-crowned triumph. Jamie consents to relinquish Jeanie, and Jeanie resolves to be a good wife to the husband who is good to her.

According to such a true and noble conclusion of the whole matter, Auld Robin Gray is an innocent victim like the others in the common calamity which has befallen them. There is no escape from it save by each sufferer trying like Jeanie to do his or her best. With that key the lock of their prison-house of circumstances is opened, and the riddle of their hapless destiny in a measure solved. The whisper is heard that "our light affliction, which is but for a moment, worketh out for us a far more exceeding, even an eternal weight of glory."

It was a grievous blunder to write a second part to "Auld Robin Gray." Lady Anne herself suspected it. It was a more grievous blunder still, as detracting from the perfect innocence of the victims, to make auld Robin the treacherous villain of the tragedy. Had the second part of "Auld Robin Gray" become popular, the world would have owed no thanks to the Laird of Dalzell for putting the idea into Lady Anne's head. It was his angry exclamation on listening to the first part of the song:

"Oh! the villain! Oh! the auld rascal! I ken wha stealt the poor cow—it was auld Robin Gray himsel'!"—which tempted her to murder her own creation by criminating Jeanie's kindly gudeman. But the world was right in never greatly favouring the second part of "Auld Robin Gray," either in part or as a whole.

If one can at all forgive the blunder of a second part, it has verses not unworthy of the author of "Auld Robin Gray." The first three verses have beauty of their own, and so have the lines which detail the theft of the cow, and the concluding verses.

> "I cared not for Crummie, I thought but o' thee—
> I thought it was Crummie stood 'twixt you and me."

> "How truth soon or late comes to open daylight!
> For Jamie cam' back, and your cheek it grew white—
> White, white grew your cheek, but aye true unto me—
> Ay, Jeanie! I'm thankfu', I'm thankfu' to dee."

> "The first days were dowie while time slipt awa',
> But saddest and sairest to Jeanie o' a'
> Was thinkin' she couldna be honest and right,
> Wi' tears in her e'e while her heart was sae light."

One hears no more of the second or third

version of this sequel, which was "from Jeanie's own lips," and which Lady Anne mentioned to Sir Walter Scott; but there is a comical French version of the original song by Florian, printed in the "Lives of the Lindsays." It begins,—

> "Quand les moutons sont dans la bergerie,
> Que le sommeil aux humains est si doux,
> Je pleure, hélas ! les chagrins de ma vie,
> Et près de moi dort mon bon vieux époux."

AULD ROBIN GRAY.

When the sheep are in the fauld, when the kye's a' at hame,
And a' the weary warld to rest are gane,
The woes o' my heart fa' in showers frae my e'e,
Unkent by my gudeman, wha sleeps sound by me.

Young Jamie lo'ed me weel, and sought me for his bride,
But saving a crown he had naething else beside;
To mak the crown a pound my Jamie gaed to sea,
And the crown and the pound—they were baith for me.

He hadna been gane a twelvemonth and a day
When my father brake his arm, and the cow was stown
    away;
My mother she fell sick—my Jamie was at sea—
And Auld Robin Gray came a-courting me.

My father couldna work, my mother couldna spin,
I toiled day and night, but their bread I couldna win;
Auld Rob maintained them baith, and, wi' tears in his e'e,
Said, "Jeanie, for their sakes, will ye no marry me?"

My heart it said na, and I looked for Jamie back,
But hard blew the winds, and his ship was a wrack;
His ship was a wrack—why didna Jamie dee?
Or why am I spared to cry, Woe is me?

My father urged me sair—my mother didna speak,
But she looket in my face till my heart was like to break;
They gied him my hand—my heart was in the sea—
And so Robin Gray he was gudeman to me.

I hadna been his wife a week but only four,
When, mournfu' as I sat on the stane at my door,
I saw my Jamie's ghaist, for I couldna think it he,
Till he said, "I'm come hame, love, to marry thee."

Oh! sair, sair did we greet, and mickle say o' a',
I gi'ed him ae kiss and bade him gang awa'.
I wish that I were dead, but I'm no like to dee,
For tho' my heart is broken, I'm young, woe's me!

I gang like a ghaist, and I carena to spin,
I darena think on Jamie, for that would be a sin;
But I'll do my best a gude wife to be,
For oh! Robin Gray he is kind to me.

SECOND PART.

The winter was come, 'twas simmer nae mair,
And, trembling, the leaves were fleeing thro' the air;
"Oh, winter," says Jeanie, " we kindly agree,
For the sun he looks wae when he shines upon me."

Nae longer she mourned, her tears were a' spent,
Despair it was come, and she thought it content—
She thought it content, but her cheek it grew pale,
And she bent like a lily broke down by the gale.

Her father and mother observed her decay;
"What ails ye, my bairn?" they ofttimes would say;
"Ye turn round your wheel, but you come little speed,
For feeble's your hand and silly's your thread."

She smiled when she heard them, to banish their fear,
But wae looks the smile that is seen through a tear,
And bitter's the tear that is forced by a love
Which honour and virtue can never approve.

Her father was vexed and her mother was wae,
But pensive and silent was auld Robin Gray;
He wandered his lane, and his face it grew lean,
Like the side of a brae where the torrent has been.

Nae questions he spiered her concerning her health,
He looked at her often, but aye 'twas by stealth;
When his heart it grew grit, and often he feigned
To gang to the door to see if it rained.

He took to his bed—nae physic he sought,
But ordered his friends all around to be brought;
While Jeanie supported his head in its place,
Her tears trickled down and fell on his face.

" Oh, greet nae mair, Jeanie," said he wi' a groan,
" I'm no worth your sorrow—the truth maun be known;
Send round for your neighbours, my hour it draws near,
And I've that to tell that it's fit a' should hear.

" I've wrong'd her," he said, " but I kent it ower late,
I've wronged her, and sorrow is speeding my date;
But a' for the best, since my death will soon free
A faithfu' young heart that was ill matched wi' me.

" I lo'ed and I courted her mony a day,
The auld folks were for me, but still she said nay;
I kentna o' Jamie, nor yet of her vow,
In mercy forgive me—'twas I stole the cow.

" I cared not for Crummie, I thought but o' thee—
I thought it was Crummie stood 'twixt you and me;
While she fed your parents, oh, did you not say
You never would marry wi' auld Robin Gray?

" But sickness at hame and want at the door—
You gied me your hand, while your heart it was sore;
I saw it was sore, why took I her hand?
Oh, that was a deed to my shame o'er the land!

" How truth soon or late comes to open daylight!
For Jamie cam' back and your cheek it grew white—
White, white grew your cheek, but aye true unto me—
Ay, Jeanie, I'm thankfu'—I'm thankfu' to dee.

" Is Jamie come here yet?" and Jamie they saw—
" I've injured you sair, lad, so leave me you may a';
Be kind to my Jeanie, and soon may it be;
Waste nae time, my dauties, in mourning for me."

They kissed his cauld hands, and a smile o'er his face
Seemed hopefu' of being accepted by grace;
" Oh, doubtna," said Jamie, " forgi'en he will be—
Wha wouldna be tempted, my love, to win thee?"

* * * * * *

The first days were dowie while time slipt awa',
But saddest and sairest to Jeanie o' a'
Was thinkin' she couldna be honest and right,
Wi' tears in her e'e while her heart was sae light.

But nae guile had she, and her sorrow away,
The wife of her Jamie the tear couldna stay;
A bonnie wee bairn—the auld folks by the fire—
Oh, now she has a' that her heart can desire.

LE VIEUX ROBIN GRAY.

Quand les moutons sont dans la bergerie,
  Que le sommeil aux humains est si doux,
Je pleure, hélas! les chagrins de ma vie,
  Et près de moi dort mon bon vieux époux.

Jame m'aimait,—pour prix de sa constance
  Il eut mon cœur; mais Jame n'avait rien;
Il s'embarqua dans la seule espérance
  A tant d'amour de joindre un peu de bien.

Après un an notre vache est volée—
  Le bras cassé mon père rentre un jour—
Ma mère était malade et désolée,
  Et Robin Gray vint me faire la cour.

Le pain manquait dans ma pauvre retraite,
  Robin nourrit mes parens malheureux.
La larme à l'œil, il me disait, " Jeannette,
  Epouse moi du moins pour l'amour d'eux!"

Je disais, " Non, pour Jame je respire;"
  Mais son vaisseau sur mer vint à périr;
Et j'ai vécu—je vis encore pour dire,
  " Malheur à moi de n'avoir pu mourir!"

Mon père alors parla du mariage—
  Sans en parler ma mère l'ordonna:

Mon pauvre cœur était mort du naufrage,
Ma main restait—mon père la donna.

Un mois après, devant ma porte assise
Je revois Jame, et je crus m'abuser.
" C'est moi," dit-il, " pourquoi tant de surprise ?
Ma chère amour, je reviens t'épouser ! "

Ah ! que de pleurs ensemble nous versâmes !
Un seul baiser, suivi d'un long soupir,
Fut notre adieu—tous deux nous répétâmes,
" Malheur à moi de n'avoir pu mourir ! "

Je ne ris plus, j'écarte de mon âme
Le souvenir d'un amant si chéri ;
Je veux tâcher d'être une bonne femme,
Le vieux Robin est un si bon mari.

CAROLINA BARONESS NAIRNE.

1766—1845.

THE grandly outlined, richly wooded Strath of the Earn, lying between the Grampians and the Ochils, with Ben Voirlich for its landmark, was verily a stronghold of Jacobite lords and lairds. Athol Murrays, Perth Drummonds, Robertsons, Oliphants, and Menzieses, were "out" either in the '74 or the '45, or in both those years of rebellion. Some of the Strath families never recovered the losses consequent on their clannish fidelity to the Stuarts and their dogged, unreasoning opposition to the House of Hanover. Highland Scotland north of the Tay was quite another country from the lowlands of Scotland south of the Forth, which had Tweedside on the right and Clydesdale on the left, and Highland Scotland had altogether different interests and associations. Trade and commerce, political freedom, and men's individual rights, had no footing in old Strathearn. Tender and true as the feudal bond might prove in honest hands, it was but a version of serfdom, with a burden of heavy evils both to chief and vassal. In Strathearn, the Roman Catholic religion lingered, and Episcopacy, abjured elsewhere, flourished here. Those battles on national questions of liberty of conscience and the rights of the Kirk, which had been fought so gallantly on many a moorland field, and in many a burgh street of the south, had never penetrated into the great northern strath, made up of wild tracts of deer forest and minor glens, each with its tributary stream, its green meadows, its hanging woods, and the castle of its local chief. Each Drummond, Murray, or Oliphant—unless, indeed, the houses were divided against themselves—thought and fought on the side of his feudal head, and that as a matter of first duty. If there were exceptions among the clansmen, the traditions of the district prove how these exceptions were regarded and with what a high hand they were put down. One well-known tradition will have it that Lord Perth shot down a man who dared to have a mind of his own on the propriety of "rising" and following Prince Charlie. Another, which refers to Lady Nairne's grandfather, asserts that some tenants of Gask having had sufficient whiggery and sagacity to object to the landing in Moidart, as foreseeing the end, the laird took steps to intimidate the pestilent fellows by prohibiting them from cutting down the ripe crops on their little farms, while the cattle were starving in the stalls.

In such a region, surrounded by such a single-handed, one-ideaed people, Carolina, Baroness Nairne, was born in 1766. She was doubly and trebly of Jacobite antecedents. The Oliphants of Gask, her father's house; the Robertsons of Strowan, her mother's house; the Nairnes of Nairne, cousins of both Oliphants and Robertsons, had every one of them been in trouble and exile. One of these Nairnes, Captain Nairne in default of the forfeited titles and estates of his ancestors, was Carolina's kinsman, lover, husband. These families had literally sailed in the same boat, having most of them escaped in one ship from the east coast of Scotland to Sweden, in the desperation of 1746. The marriages of cousins once and again, as in the alliances of royal houses, had rendered more stringent and inveterate the hereditary cast of mind. Carolina Oliphant's father and mother were married at Versailles, when the Oliphants and the Robertsons were still attached to the court of St. Germains. The couple were soon enabled to return home; but Carolina was a blooming girl of eighteen before her grandfather and grandmother, on the Robertsons' side, had their outlawry removed, and were suffered, by the clemency of a German George, to exchange their banishment at Givet for their own house at Strowan. These circumstances might have had the effect of introducing a foreign element into the characters of the brave, fair, and witty partisans of the Chevalier de St. George and Charles Edward; but it does not seem that the Oliphants imbibed much French culture. Like the earlier Stuarts and the later Bourbons, they came back as they had gone away, having learnt nothing and forgotten nothing. They were Jacobites of the Jacobites, chiefs and aristocrats of the purest water, with all the virtues and all the faults of such a creed and calling.

Carolina Oliphant, in her songs for the people, vindicated nobly the genuine humanity of true nobility, and the strong, sweet sympathies of a patriarchal life. But Carolina Oliphant also was a grand dame. The blue blood in her veins ran very blue. In her stateliness as a bride, she put aside with some impatience and vexation the kiss of her cousin and bridegroom, as being too bold and public an assertion of the rights which she had just given him. She had even a greater horror than Lady Anne Lindsay cherished of being reduced to the level of literary publicity, and of being exposed to rude praise and blame along with the common herd of authors. Not only was she a woman,—and authorship was counted unfeminine by these great ladies,—she was also a lady, an Oliphant, a Nairne. Lady Nairne did not so much as confide to Lord Nairne the secret which would have made his heart proud, if he were a match for his wife in genius and feeling. She did not even tell him that she was the author of "The Land o' the Leal," lest his honest gratification should tempt him to betray the truth. We dwell under another régime now, and the bluest blood runs warm and kind; for the Queen of the land does not fear to put her private Journal with her name attached to it into her people's hands, in right royal frankness and simplicity.

The quaintly picturesque old house of Gask is built on a brae above the Earn, with a bonnie "burnie" wandering and winding close by, among the groves and wildernesses of ancient landscape gardening. More than a century ago, a lock of Prince Charlie's hair, his bonnet, spurs, cockade, and crucifix, were cherished there as dearest relics. The "auld laird," Carolina's father, obstinately repudiated any acknowledgment of the Elector of Hanover as sovereign of these realms. He dismissed an English clergyman who, on the death of Charles Edward, took the oath of allegiance to George III., from officiating as chaplain at Gask. The laird even then continued to cling to the gown and cardinal's hat of Cardinal Stewart, at Rome,—wildly, wilfully hoping that they might yet be merged into a crown and coronation robes when the priest should sit on the British throne as Henry IX. In return, King George, who could afford to be good-natured, sent this message through the member for Perthshire:—"The Elector of Hanover's compliments to the Laird of Gask, and wishes to tell him how much the Elector respects the Laird for the steadiness of his principles."

We first hear of Carolina as named in fond fanaticism for the gallant, but frail hero of her house. She was "sturdy little Car" when two years old, and her mother speaks of her having been taken for a space from the Gask nursery, and "sitting on a chair as prim as any there at the reading, this evening being Sunday." Carolina was the third of a family of six children, four daughters and two sons. Marjory, or "Maj," and Amelia were her seniors, and "Laurie," the young laird, Margaret, and Charles, her juniors. The children had the misfortune to lose their mother when "little Car" was only eight years of age. "Lady Gask's" last speech to her bairns was beautiful in its motherly, wifely kindness:— "See which will be the best bairn and stay longest with papa." Lady Gask's place was supplied in a degree, first, by old Lady Gask, the children's grandmother on the father's side, and then by their grandmother's sister, the young Oliphants' grand-aunt, Miss Henrietta Nairne. The girls had a Mrs. Cramond from Perth for their governess, to impart to them the practice of "ye needle, principles of religion, and loyalty, a good carriage, and talking tolerable good English," with the remuneration of from ten to twelve guineas a-year. A "fiddler," foreign evidently, a Mr. Marconchi, came out also once a week to Gask, that the young people might get their dancing lessons, and possibly music lessons, on the harpsichord or guitar. In the latter branch of polite education, "little Car," who had developed into "pretty Miss

Car" of the schoolroom, was an adept and enthusiast, her taste and skill winning the approbation of Niel Gow, himself the king of Scotch fiddlers. "Pretty Miss Car" passed soon into a county belle and beauty, styled in the sentimentality of the day "the Flower of Strathearn." She was tall in figure and dignified in gait, had dark eyes and hair, an aquiline nose, and small mouth. Her arms and hands were fine. Her portrait painted, in middle life, by Watson Gordon, gives the idea of an aristocratic beauty, sensitive but self-controlled. Her sister, writing of Lady Nairne's appearance in advanced age, remarked that she was still "very *distingué* in brow and nose."

There was ample scope for the gaieties and the conquests of a county belle in the country houses—mostly those of kinsmen as well as of friends—around Gask. These houses were occupied by resident lairds' families for almost the entire year. The marriages of Carolina Oliphant's elder sisters to two loyal Stewarts—lairds of neighbouring glens—widened the family ties. Two additional homes were added to that of her grandfather, the restored Laird of Strowan, where Carolina was the young lady, the pride and darling of the house. The departure of her elder sisters to houses of their own, left her, "to the manner born" as she was, the elegant and lively mistress of Gask. For her surroundings at this period, and for the kind of festivity in which she joined, Lady Nairne has herself supplied us with an animated hint in her "County Meeting."

> "Ye're welcome, leddies, ane and a',
> Ye're welcome to our County Ha';
> Sae weel ye look when buskit braw
>   To grace our County Meeting!
> An', gentlemen, ye're welcome too,
> In waistcoats white and tartan too,
> Gae seek a partner, mak' yer bow,
>   Syne dance our County Meeting.

> "Ah, weel dune now, there's auld Sir John,
> Wha aye maun lead the dancin' on,
> An' Leddy Bet, wi' her turban prim,
> An' wee bit velvet 'neath her chin;
> See how they nimbly, nimbly go!
> While youngsters follow in a row,
> Wi' mony a belle an' mony a beau,
>   To dance our County Meeting.

"There's the Major, and his sister too,
  He in the bottle-green, she in the blue;
  (Some years sin' syne that gown was new
    At our County Meeting.)
They are a worthy canty pair,
An' unco proud o' their nephew Blair,
O' sense or siller he's nae great share,
    Tho' he's the King o' the Meeting.

"An' there's our member, and provost Whig,
  Our doctor in his yellow wig,
  Wi' his fat wife, wha taks a jig
    Aye at our County Meeting.
Miss Betty, too, I see her there,
Wi' her sonsy face and bricht red hair,
Dancin' till she can dance nae mair
    At our County Meeting.

"There's beauty Bell wha a' surpasses,
  An' heaps o' bonnie country lasses,
  Wi' the heiress o' the Gowdenlea—
    Folk say she's unco dorty.
Lord Bawbee aye he's lookin' there,
An' sae is the Major and Major's heir,
Wi' the Laird, the Shirra, an' mony mair,
    I could reckon them to forty.

"See Major O'Neill has got her hand,
  An' in the dance they've ta'en their stand
  ('Impudence comes frae Paddy's land,'
    Say the lads o' our County Meeting);

But ne'er ye fash, gang thro' the reel,
The country-dance, ye dance sae weel,
An' ne'er let waltz or dull quadrille
    Spoil our County Meeting.

" Afore we end, strike up the spring
O' Thulichan and Hieland fling,
The Haymakers and Bumpkin fine,
    At our County Meeting.
Gow draws his bow, folk haste away,
While some are glad and some are wae,
A' blithe to meet some ither day
    At our County Meeting."

And was not the trouble in "Jamie the Laird"— a county belle's dilemma—perhaps a leaf from the lady's own experience?—

" Send a horse to the water, ye'll no mak him drink;
Send a fule to the college, ye'll no mak him think;
Send a craw to the singin', an' still he will craw;
An' the wee laird had nae rummelgumshion ava.
Yet he is the pride o' his fond mother's e'e,
In body or mind nae faut can she see;
' He's a fell clever lad an' a bonnie wee man,'
Is aye the beginnin' an' end o' her sang.
    An' oh! she's a haverin' Lucky, I trow,
    An' oh! she's a haverin' Lucky, I trow.
' He's a fell clever lad an' a bonnie wee man,'
Is aye the beginnin' an' end o' her sang.

"His legs they are bowed, his een they do glee,
His wig, whiles it's aff, and when on it's agee,
He's braid as he's lang, an' ill-faur'd is he,
A dafter like body I never did see.
An' yet for this crator she says I am deein';
When that I deny, she's fear'd at my leein';
Obliged to put up wi' this sair defamation,
I'm liken to dee wi' grief an' vexation.
  An' oh ! she's a haverin' Lucky, etc.

  *   *   *   *   *

"Frien's, gie yer advice, I'll follow yer counsel,
Maun I speak to the provost or honest town-council?
Or the writers, or lawyers, or doctors? now say;
For the law on the Lucky I shall an' will hae.
The hale town at me are jibin' an' joerin',
For a leddy like me it's really past bearin'.
The Lucky maun now hae done wi' her claverin',
For I'll no put up wi' her nor her haverin';
  For oh ! she's a randy, I trow, I trow,
  For oh ! she's a randy, I trow, I trow.
'He's a fell clever lad an' a bonnie wee man,'
Is aye the beginnin' an' end o' her sang."

In these days Carolina Oliphant had her share of suitors; but she early pledged herself (impelled by characteristic motives of proud devotion, disinterestedness, and decision) to wait for the promotion of her cousin, Captain Nairne, who was nine years her senior, in order to become the wife of a landless soldier of fortune.

The arch-Jacobite chief, her father, whom Carolina has painted with tender touches as "the auld laird" of one of her best songs, "The Auld House," died, full of years, and of the deserved regard of his children and his people, on the New Year's Day of 1792, when Carolina was twenty-five years of age.

A year later, while Carolina still presided over the house of Gask—now her eldest brother Laurence's house—he celebrated his accession by a dinner to his tenantry, and sang to them a new version of an old Scotch ditty, "The Ploughman," by an unknown author. This song is stated to have been Carolina Oliphant's first attempt in the art of song-writing; and the inducement to the attempt has received an explanation. She already knew and appreciated Robert Burns as a poet, and she had induced her brother, the laird, to subscribe for one of the earlier editions of his poems. She had an especial interest in those gems of song which he was setting to old admired airs, and which had been previously spoilt by being unworthily linked to gross or mean words.

Driving through a country fair near Gask, Carolina Oliphant saw in the hands of many of the people a common song-book, which as she judged, was full of coarseness and folly. Such song-books had long been the lighter literature of the people, and she was fired with the ambition of becoming in her turn a purifier of Scotch songs. She would do it in strictest secrecy, preserving her aristocratic and womanly reserve unbroken; and, while utterly unknown as an author, she would aid in raising the standard of taste and morals in the rustic world. The motive was honourable to authorship; and Carolina Oliphant, while she remained, as she wished, a nameless bard for at least one generation, had the reward which she prized for its intrinsic worth. She divided largely with Burns the gracious honour of rewriting many old songs, so that they came home to thousands of hearts, refining and elevating them. But, while Carolina Oliphant's indifference, and even aversion to the fame of authorship is patent, her voluntary acceptance of so difficult a task is not in harmony with the assumption of "excessive diffidence," as the cause of her persistent secrecy in writing.

Carolina is supposed to have set herself first to the writing of merry and humorous songs. Probably to this period belong her "John Tod" and her inimitable "Laird of Cockpen." Naturally, too, she at once took to the inditing of spirited and pathetic Jacobite songs. It must be taken into consideration, with regard to the latter, that the Jacobite creed was not far-fetched and fantastic to Carolina Oliphant. Her hero-worship of poor Prince Charlie might be inconsistent with her autocratical condemnation of whatever offended her principles and taste in the old ballads and in the writings of Burns; but it did not so strike her mind, which was fine rather than broad, and did not easily free itself from hereditary prejudices. The delight of her old grandfather of Strowan in the revival and graphic embodiment of the memories of his youth, would suffice to make Jacobitism, after its last hope had died out in ashes, a real and still present power to Carolina Oliphant. Thus her Jacobite songs are not affected, or elaborate with meretricious ornament, or overlaid with mock sentiment. They are among the last of the earnest Jacobite songs. They are almost as earnest as those written at the era of the Rebellion. They are spontaneous lyrics, possessing unity and fire, and true and simple feeling.

But whether Carolina Oliphant's songs were patriotic, in her sense of the word, or purely sportive, she was happily busy with her self-imposed task. In the midst of her duties as the mistress of a hospitable Highland country house, and her gaieties as an acknowledged county toast, she sat and wrote often and long at her desk. She remained silent as to what she wrote. She was eminently a woman who could keep her own counsel, and, by the spell of her birth, breeding, beauty, and wit, could ward off every unauthorised approach to her confidence. Her intimate friends imagined that she was busy writing letters to her cousin, Captain Nairne, to whom it was always "*understood*" that she was engaged in marriage.

Three years after her father's death, when

Carolina was twenty-nine, her brother Laurence married the heiress of Ardblair. Carolina was thus called to vacate her post for a successor. But, owing to Captain Nairne's long-delayed promotion, the completion of the cousins' engagement was not yet possible, and Carolina continued to reside with her brother and his wife.

The Laird of Gask had joined the Perthshire Light Dragoons, one of the militia regiments raised to defend the country from mob anarchy during the alarm of Jacobinism, which had come in the room of Jacobitism. In 1797, just as the French Revolution was at its height, the regiment was ordered to quarters in the North of England, and Carolina accompanied the laird and the new lady to Durham. Of the family's residence there a highly romantic, slightly cock-and-bull tradition exists. It is said that Carolina Oliphant, in the mature charms of her thirty-second year, attended a ball at Sunderland, where a Royal Duke—not a Stuart—was present. He was her partner, and became so enamoured of the fair and gifted daughter of a rebel Highland laird, that only the lady's pre-engaged affections and the Royal Marriage Act saved the gentleman from the terrible indiscretion of laying his ducal coronet at her feet. Is not this story a late edition of that verse of the modernised ballad of "Mally Lee," which caps all Mally's perfections by a triumphant assertion of the fact that

> " A duke cam' out frae Holyrood,
> An' danced wi' Mally Lee."

Carolina Oliphant's dancing days were nearly over. She was past her first youth, and we may believe that that high heart of hers, which would not confess its weakness, knew its own bitterness, and was sick with hope deferred. Her younger brother, Charles Oliphant, a handsome, bigoted lad, had persisted in shutting himself out from filling an office under government by refusing to take the abjuration oath. In the same year, 1797, he went abroad, and after drooping in health for some time, died in early manhood at Paris. Another loss by death struck Carolina, in striking one of the few intimate friends for whom her concentrated attachments were strong and lasting. This was the death of the first-born and dearly-loved child of Mrs. Campbell Colquhoun —the same Mary Anne Erskine who, while keeping house for her brother William in Edinburgh, had been on very sisterly terms with another advocate, "Earl Walter." It was in reference to this "bonnie bairn's" death, and with the intention of consoling the mother, that Caroline wrote and forwarded to Mrs. Campbell Colquhoun (at the same time binding her not to divulge the authorship) the one perfect Scottish hymn, "The Land o' the Leal."

The Oliphants returned to Scotland. While Carolina's mind was sobered, and her heart softened, by her own griefs and those of her friends, she happened to go on a visit to a neighbouring country house. An English clergyman was of the party, and preached on one occasion. His sermon deeply impressed a listener who was in circumstances to render her peculiarly susceptible to tender and devout influences. It seemed to her that she then definitely and permanently laid hold of the hope set before her; and she continued to look back on the season as that of her spiritual awakening.

Carolina Oliphant dwelt at Gask with her brother and sister-in-law till 1806, when Captain Nairne at last got the brevet-rank of major, and was appointed Assistant Inspector-General of Barracks in Scotland. The constant couple were married during the same summer by the family chaplain, in the new house of Gask. The bride was in her forty-first year, the bridegroom hard on fifty; but bride and bridegroom called for honour, and not pity, since they were of the grain in which loyalty flourishes green and unfading. Carolina Oliphant only shared the fate of the most winning of George III.'s princesses. Pretty, gentle Princess Mary, in the bloom and grace of her twentieth year, won the heart of her cousin William of Gloucester, and gave him her own in return. But the exigencies of the country demanded that Duke William should remain unwedded until the baby Princess Charlotte, heiress of the throne, was grown to womanhood, and satisfactorily disposed of in marriage to a Protestant prince. So Princess Mary and Duke William served for each other by that hardest service of waiting—not seven years, but seven and seven again. Immediately after the gala wedding of young Princess Charlotte and Prince Leopold, there was another wedding, quiet, almost private,—like that celebrated in the upper room of the new house of Gask,—between Princess Charlotte's aunt and Princess Charlotte's father's cousin. These cousins' marriages, whether in a royal palace or at Gask, had crushed out of them, by the "weary weight" of years, much of the glory and gladness which would have attended on their celebration when brides and bridegrooms were in their prime. Well for both that the true love which is immortal had not failed or swerved aside from youth to middle age, and was still their sure foundation.

Major Nairne is said by Lady Nairne's friends to have been the hero of the two following songs of his wife's :—

KIND ROBIN LO'ES ME.

Robin is my ain gudeman,
Now match him, carlins, gin ye can,
For ilk ane whitest thinks her swan,
   But kind Robin lo'es me.
     *   *   *   *

Robin he comes hame at e'en
Wi' pleasure glancin' in his een,
He tells me a' he's heard and seen,
   An' syne how he lo'es me.
There's some hae land and some hae gowd,
An' mair wad hae them gin they could,
But a' I wish o' warld's gude
   Is Robin aye to lo'e me.

O WEEL'S ME ON MY AIN MAN.

O weel's me on my ain man,
My ain man, my ain man,
O weel's me on my ain gudeman,
   He'll aye be welcome hame.

I'm wae I blamed him yesternicht,
For now my heart is feather licht;
For gowd I wadna gie the sicht,
I see him linkin' ower the hicht.
   O weel's me, &c.

Rin, Jeanie, bring the kebbuck ben,
An' fin' aneath the speckled hen;

> Meg, rise and sweep aboot the fire,
> Syne cry on Johnnie frae the byre.
> For weel's me on my ain man,
> My ain man, my ain man,
> For weel's me on my ain gudeman!
> I see him linkin' hame.

If Lady Nairne thus made a compromise with her reserve, and expressed her thoughts and feelings in lowly guise in order to do honour to her husband, the by-play is suggestive—not only of the pride which thus found an excuse for venting its woman's weakness, but of the relief which rank and state have sought in aping humility and rusticity. Thus poor Marie Antoinette retired with her court and courtiers from magnificent Versailles, to get up a mock pastoral of village life at little Trianon.

Major Nairne and his wife resided, by necessity, in Edinburgh. Her old childless grandfather, the Laird of Strowan, had built for his nephew and his grand-daughter in the suburbs a cottage, named, in compliment to Mrs. Nairne, Carolina Cottage. There Carolina Nairne's only child, a son, was born in 1808.

Major and Mrs. Nairne lived in Edinburgh in great retirement. This could not have been entirely from motives of wise economy, since their income was more than sufficient for the small household, and visiting was then a much less expensive process than it is now. The fact was, that at the most literary epoch of the old capital, its society had few attractions for the Highland and Jacobite lady, who had been accustomed to reign as a queen in Strathearn, and to count on the regard of princes and their court—albeit they were banished princes and a mock court. Edinburgh lawyers—though Walter Scott was one of them, and Carolina Nairne's friend, Mary Anne Erskine, had married another—formed a different order of society from that to which Mrs. Nairne had been accustomed. Anne Grant of Laggan, the writer of

"Oh where, and oh where does your Highland laddie dwell?"

was a Highlander, and might dwell within a little distance of Carolina Cottage; Elizabeth Hamilton, planning her works of charity and crooning her "Ain Fireside," could not live far off; and Joanna Baillie might come and go to and from Castle Street, exciting some enthusiasm, yet there existed an insurmountable barrier between these women and the woman who, in her songs, showed the kindliness of her common nature, deep down beneath the piled-up obstacles of partisanship and exclusiveness. The inevitable result of such contraction could not be anything else than the production of narrowness and dogmatism, even in a soul naturally generous and high-minded in the best sense.

Among the exceptions which Carolina Nairne made (and it ought to be said, that when she opened her heart it must have been with frankness, simplicity, and rare tenderness) were the Keiths of Ravelston, the old friends and kindred of Sir Walter Scott and Mrs. Cockburn. The Keiths were at this time represented by a hospitable, eccentric elderly brother and sister, who became also family connections of Mrs. Nairne through the marriage of her younger sister Margaret with the brother, the laird of Ravelston. At the Saturday parties at Ravelston, with its stately homeliness and obstinate conservatism, the daughter of Gask and granddaughter of Strowan was in her element. To members of the county families, neighbours of the Keiths, and especially to one—a young girl with the divine gift of song—the dignified and still beautiful matron was gracious and winning.

The Misses Hume, daughters of Baron Hume, were likewise admitted on intimate terms into the very small and select circle in which Mrs. Nairne moved. These ladies had an important influence on her history where the public are concerned. At the head of the musical society of Edinburgh were the Misses Hume. They were consulted by Mr. Purdie, music dealer, when he proposed, about 1821, to bring out a collection of national airs with suitable words. The Misses Hume consulted in turn their friend Mrs. Nairne, with whose own aspirations the scheme fitted in admirably. The result was the formation of a ladies' committee, the proceedings of which were meant to be shrouded in mystery, and were really long kept in concealment. The members of this committee either supplied Mr. Purdie's songs or revised them. It is almost unnecessary to say that the presiding genius was Carolina Nairne. No doubt literary puzzles were the fashion of the era, but this well-born and accomplished little clique, who professed, and in general were fully disposed to despise fashions which they themselves did not set, strike the work-a-day men and women of the present generation as being half-supercilious, half-childish in their mummery. Mrs. Nairne assumed the not very euphonious name of Mrs. Bogan of Bogan, and used the non-aristocratic alliterative initials of B. B., in her dealings with the publisher. (Perhaps there was a little humorous hit at her own conscious predilections in the choice of name and initials.) Even this *nom de plume* was whispered charily to Mr. Purdie under the seal of utmost secrecy. Its owner was so much in earnest in her disguise, that she wrote in a feigned hand, and employed other feigned hands to transcribe her MSS. These MSS. she signed variously "B. B.," or "sent by B. B.," or merely "S. M.," the initials of "Scottish Minstrel," the title which Mr. Purdie and the ladies of the committee had given to the collection. At a later date she wished to shake the evidence that it was a woman who had composed her songs, and writes to one of the committee: "As you observed, the more mystery the better, and still the balance is in favour of 'the lords of the creation.' I cannot help in some degree undervaluing beforehand what is said to be a feminine production." The last sentence is very characteristic of Carolina Nairne and her age. She ventured, however, on personal interviews with Mr. Purdie, at his place of business, as Mrs. Bogan of Bogan. On these occasions she was carefully got up for the occasion as an old country lady of a former generation. One can imagine the dash of fun and frolic with which the former county belle and beauty would engage in this species of masquerading, whether or not she borrowed the idea from the clever mystifications practised with success by Miss Graham Stirling on Scott and Jeffrey. Mrs. Nairne was likewise so successful that Mr. Purdie never dreamed of Mrs. Bogan of Bogan being a lady resident in the same town with himself, and associated with anything so patent to his senses as Edinburgh Castle.

The "Scottish Minstrel," to which Carolina Nairne contributed largely in songs which would have become famous and far-spread in any language, was completed in six octavo volumes in 1824.

In the course of the publication, and in the delight which B. B.'s songs inspired, there were many questions asked with respect to the author. Some of these were even put in Carolina Nairne's presence. She declared long afterwards that she had not "the Author of Waverley's" tact in parrying a question, neither had she the refined sauciness by which Lady Anne Lindsay turned the tables on her assailants. But Carolina Nairne could be silent; and when it was her pleasure to be silent, he or she must have been a bold man or woman who would have pressed her with unrestrained curiosity.

Another work which the committee of gentle ladies thought of taking up, fortunately fell to the ground. This was to lay daringly decorous hands on Burns's songs, and purify them.

During the publication of the "Scottish Minstrel," George IV. visited Scotland. It was a great event to the nation; and among other accompaniments, "Glengarry and his tail" formed the last truly Highland spectacle in the picturesque, eagerly-thronged streets of Edinburgh. At the levee in Holyrood, Major Nairne's relative, the Duke of Athole, presented the major to the King, in late submission to the House of Hanover. Other descendants of attainted nobles took the opportunity to offer their tardy homage. Sir Walter Scott prepared a memorial for them, praying for the removal of the forfeitures of their titles. George, who was not destitute of the earlier German Georges' clemency, received the petition in very good part, and a Bill was passed in 1824 reversing many attainders. Among them was that of the baron's rank of Lord Nairne, which dated from the reign of Charles I., and to which Major Nairne was the heir and immediate successor. Thus Carolina Nairne became a peeress worthy of the honour. But the estate of Nairne, in Strath

Ard, Perthshire, which had been purchased by
the Athole Murrays after the '45, was irrevocably lost to the representatives of its original
owners. The House of Nairne had been destroyed by James, Duke of Athole, to the indignation of the outlawed Lord Nairne and his son.
The belfry—the solitary relic of it which was
preserved—had been presented to the town of
Perth, where it surmounted King James's Hospital. It was, therefore, a barren honour and a
landless lairdship which was restored to Carolina
Nairne and her husband. But, with their old
Scottish pride of birth and rank, it was a sacred
privilege to them only to bear the title, though
it had been borne begging their bread. The
mockery of the empty distinction was better
realised by their son, William, sixth and last
Lord Nairne, who visited Nairne in 1834, when
he was in his twenty-seventh year, and "spoke
mournfully of the reverses of his house." Doubtless he stood by the Bell-tree, and speculated
on what might have been, if the Lord Nairne
of the '45 had not there marshalled his tenants
and servants, and marched them to fight under

the standard of Prince Charlie; and if the same Prince Charlie, the idol of Carolina Baroness Nairne's romantic imagination, had not dined and slept a night, in his descent from Blair, under that roof-tree of which there was not then a rafter or a stone remaining.

When Lord and Lady Nairne got back their ancestral title, he was in his sixty-sixth and she in her fifty-seventh year; while their son, who was educated privately and with extreme care, was a lad of fourteen years.

Lady Nairne in middle life spent much of her leisure, not only in writing, but in drawing and painting, for which she seems to have had a marked taste.

In 1830 occurred the first of the grievous breaches in Lady Nairne's household. Lord Nairne died at the age of seventy-four. Her son, a delicate lad, a little past his majority, was already showing symptoms of premature decline. In place of entering a profession, he was fain to seek more vigorous health from a milder climate. Lady Nairne has verses on leaving Edinburgh, in which there is a pleasant summary of its traits, as they struck her, and a reference to "departed joys," in her case "never to return."

"Fareweel, Edinburgh, where happy we hae been,
Fareweel, Edinburgh, Caledonia's queen ;
Auld Reekie, fare ye weel, and Reekie New beside,
Ye're like a chieftain grim and gray wi' a young bonnie bride.

"Fareweel, Edinburgh, and your trusty Volunteers,
Your Council a' sae circumspect, your Provost without peers,
Your stately College, stuff'd wi' lear, your rantin' High-Schule yard,
The jibe, the lick, the roguish trick, the ghaists o' th' auld town guard.

"Fareweel, Edinburgh, your philosophic men,
Your scribes that set you a' to richts and wield the golden pen,
The Session-court, your thrang resort, big-wigs and lang gowns a';
An' if ye dinna keep the peace, it's no for want o' law.

"Fareweel, Edinburgh, and a' your glittering wealth,
Your Bernard's Well, your Calton Hill, where every breeze is health ;
An', spite o' a' your fresh sea-gales, should ony chance to dee,
It's no for want o' recipe, the doctor, or the fee.

"Fareweel, Edinburgh, your hospitals and ha's,
The rich man's friend, the Cross long kenned, auld ports and city wa's,
The kirks that grace their honoured place now peacefu' as they stand,
Where'er they're found, on Scottish ground, the bulwarks o' the land.

"Fareweel, Edinburgh, your sons o' genius fine,
That send your name on wings o' fame beyond the burning line—
A name that's stood maist since the flood, and just when it's forgot
Your bard will be forgotten too, your ain Sir Walter Scott.

"Fareweel, Edinburgh, and a' your daughters fair,
Your palace in the sheltered glen, your castle in the air,
Your rocky brows, your grassy knowes, and eke your mountains bauld,
Were I to tell your beauties a', my tale would ne'er be tauld.

"Now fareweel, Edinburgh, where happy we hae been,
Fareweel, Edinburgh, Caledonia's queen;
Prosperity to Edinburgh wi' every risin' sun,
And blessin's be on Edinburgh till Time his race has run."

Seven years of Lady Nairne's widowhood at this period of life were spent in changing her residence from place to place, hoping against hope in the fruitless effort to retain her last earthly treasure. From Clifton she went to Ireland, the country of the lad's father's birth, which his mother, from old associations and dear regard for every thing that had concerned her husband, greatly wished to visit. In Ireland the Nairnes moved from Kingston to Enniskerry. A year or two later the mother and the son proceeded from Ireland to the continent. They were accompanied by Lady Nairne's widowed and childless sister, Mrs. Keith, of Ravelston, and by a niece of the two sisters. The party travelled in turn through France (still homelike to them from many an exile's story), Italy, Switzerland, Germany, and Belgium, until they reached Brussels, where the end came. Lord Nairne had been attacked by influenza, which his weakened constitution was unable to resist. This rapidly developed chest complaint, and he died at Brussels in December, 1837, in his thirtieth year. He had given his mother the assurance which she most prized, that her hope was his hope, her Saviour his Saviour. The consolation was great; but the blow was desolating to the mourner in her seventy-second year. Relations and attendants wrote and spoke of her fortitude and resignation. It might be, however, that the checked and restrained feelings did not find fit relief. When Spring came, and the saddened travellers, leaving their charge in the churchyard at Brussels, went on without him to Munich, Salzburg, and Nice, there was no lightening of her heavy heart. Lady Nairne could keep the anchor of her soul fixed sure and steadfast in a better world; but she had drifted away from faith in any good in this world. She expresses a forlorn, almost austere, indifference to the works of genius and the beauties of scenery, which she then saw and dwelt among for the first time. She could rejoice in her dead son's gain, and cling to her remaining friends, but her own words, written more than a year after her son's death, are—"I have not the smallest pleasure in scenery or anything external, but I know that all things are working together for good." Again, some months later, she declares —"What I have seen I could once have enjoyed thoroughly, but once is enough for this world, and it is time that enthusiasm about its enjoyments be over. To me they exist no longer, and I can give thanks that so it is."

Another view, more ascetic than Christian, though it is entertained by many Christians, was cherished by Lady Nairne, and was calculated to throw a gloomy chill over the very memories of her beloved dead. It is a view which has its foundation in a forced and literal rendering, separately from the context, of one or two sentences of the Lord's, and is only consistently carried out in the monastic war with family ties. The argument is that God is jealous of the tender human affections He has given us, and strikes down their objects as being idols in the temples of our hearts. A strange interpretation this of the dealings of Him who gave back her son to the widow of Nain, and their brother to the sisters of Bethany. But, judging according to this interpretation, Lady Nairne decides, "For my own part my weaning has been such that I rejoice in the rapid lapse of days, months, and years even more than when, a too happy wife and mother, I eagerly wished the continuance of domestic happiness—a plain proof of the necessity of heavenly discipline, which has not been withheld." This creed is not rare; but it is the effect of the Bible read in the dim light of the cloister, rather than in the broad light of God's sun and the warm gleam of household hearths.

Working for charitable bazaars and devotional

reading were thenceforth Lady Nairne's chief employments. She continued abroad, at Pau and in Paris, for two or three years longer. While in Paris in 1842 she mentions, with some indignation, in a letter home, "A Scotch lady here, whom I never met, is so good as among perfect strangers to denounce me as the origin of the 'Land o' the Leal.' I cannot trace it, but very much dislike, as ever, any kind of publicity."

Nearly a year later Lady Nairne and her sister, Mrs. Keith, were still in Paris. The latter wrote home to try and "find out" in what quarter of Père-la-Chaise their dear brother Laurence had been buried twenty-four years before, and in what street he had died—a pathetic enough token that human affections vindicate their divine source, and will not be extinguished, though they may be crushed, by a morbid and false theory of the sin and the danger of their indulgence.

In 1843, when Lady Nairne was in her seventy-eighth year, this brother Laurence's son and heir affectionately urged his aunt to return to the home of her youth at Gask. She had given him a half-jesting promise that she would come and spend the last of her days under his roof, so soon as he had provided it with a mistress. Lady Nairne had thought that her own health had been benefited by a milder climate; and, like Naomi, she had shrunk from returning

<blockquote>"With empty arms and treasure lost."</blockquote>

to her country, which she had left comparatively a rich woman. But she was also a brave woman; and the kindly entreaties of her nephew, who with his wife crossed the Channel to be her escort home, at last prevailed. The same year found Lady Nairne again at Gask, looking down once more on familiar woods and waters, and away to well-known moors and deer-forests. Everything, as she said, led her back to her earlier years; and what had passed between her first and last abode at Gask seemed like "a mixed and wonderful dream." "Yet," she added gratefully, "mercy and truth have followed me all the days of my life." She liked to hear of the poor people whose grandfathers she remembered; and she took an interest in the divisions which preceded a great crisis in the Kirk of Scotland, identifying herself a good deal with the Free Kirk side of the question, though she lived and died a member of the Episcopal Church.

During the winter after her return to Scotland, she suffered from a stroke of palsy, which she bore with her accustomed firmness and calmness, emphatically setting forth her peace and joy in the prospect of death, and the simple grounds of her faith. She survived two years longer, much enduring and patient in her infirmities, the bitterness of bereavement and death alike being past. She was able to pay one visit to Edinburgh, when she went and saw those who survived of the ladies of the committee that had prepared the "Scottish Minstrel," her interest in Scottish song, it is said, having never failed. She devoted a portion of these last months to writing and receiving numerous letters with regard to the disposal of funds which her son's death had placed in her hands. She laid out the money largely on such charities as met with her approval, making the single condition that the gifts should be administered anonymously. The Oliphants were always free givers. Carolina's grandfather, out of the precarious income that reached him in his exile, had sent home a liberal donation to his poor, whom he had helped unwittingly to ruin. His son, again, had forbidden *his* sons to touch the inheritance of their grandfather Strowan, reckoning that it would descend more honourably to the clan Donnochy or Robertson. Carolina was no unworthy daughter of the chivalrous "auld laird." A few months subsequent to her death, Dr. Chalmers, for whom she had much respect and admiration, was at liberty to announce that he had received from Lady Nairne, with strict injunctions to secrecy, the sum of £300 for his West Port scheme.

On the 25th of October, 1845, Lady Nairne was out in her garden-chair in the grounds of Gask; but on the following day there was an alarming change in her state of health. On the 27th, speechless but still conscious, she listened with satisfaction to hymns and verses of Scripture which were read for her consolation and encouragement. On the same day she passed to her rest, aged seventy-nine years. She was buried in the grounds of Gask, on the site of what had been the old parish kirk, surrounded by the old kirkyard, and what is now an Episcopal chapel, founded by her nephew and herself. Her nephew lies beside her. Her native woods wave round her, the Earn "rows on" within sound, while within sight tower the Grampians.

Lady Nairne had consented that her songs should be published in a volume, without her name, but died during the preparation of the work. Her surviving sister and representative, Mrs. Keith, considering that death had removed the obstacle, put her sister's name to the volume, which was entitled "Lays of Strathearn."

Almost in spite of herself, Lady Nairne thus belongs to the world, in being identified with a people's songs. The high-born woman of the old *régime*, between whom and other men and women there existed a lofty wall, is constrained to vindicate her jealously-guarded woman's nature, and show how true was her instinctive penetration, how intensely human her sympathies.

It has been already noticed that there is a resemblance between Lady Nairne's songs and those of Susanna Blamire. There is this difference, however, that while the latter is happier in graphically describing scenes with which she herself was intimately acquainted, Lady Nairne was more successful in idealising, at some distance, the gladness and the sadness of the masses, or of the typical representatives of parties and classes among her countrymen. The exceptions to this statement are to be found in those lively, loving songs which are said to have been prompted by Lady Nairne's wifely affection; and in the noble, thrilling protest, sent home from abroad, when the writer was in her seventy-sixth year, "Would you be Young again?" we have a brave Christian contradiction to the half pagan and wholly sensuous glorification of youth, which is the popular sentiment of such a strain as Herrick's "Gather ye Rosebuds while ye may."

Both Lady Nairne and Susanna Blamire failed, naturally, in the artistic concentration and finish which Joanna Baillie could give to her songs. But while they were women far less broad in nature and culture, their songs have more personal humour or pathos, and more individual feeling. For that reason they frequently make a deeper impression.

Lady Nairne's songs extend over so wide a range that it is here impossible to analyse even the chief of them separately. She had a practice of taking well-known names and airs the sentiments of whose words offended her, or with respect to which it merely struck her fancy to supply them with fresh words or a fresh turn to former words. She dealt thus not only with names and airs of remote origin the words to which, saving for their antiquarian interest, had no charm; but also with more modern ones, some of Burns's among them. There can be no doubt that this unceremonious practice, confusing the public as to the identity of songs which were already well-known, greatly aided Lady Nairne in mystifying her generation and preserving her concealment.

Dr. Rogers, the editor of the lately published life of Lady Nairne, has with great zeal and diligence collected and assigned to her many sets of Scottish songs which were not previously recognised as her work. The present writers remember to have heard these very generally sung without the singers having the least idea of their author. At the same time the adaptation of fragments of old ballads (as in "Huntingtower" and "The Lass o' Gowrie"), and of more modern songs (as in "Auld lang syne" and "Gude nicht, and joy be wi' you a'") has rendered it difficult to apportion Lady Nairne's share of merit (certainly a great one) in the case of many songs. There are songs which, from the name and theme downwards, are Lady Nairne's own. Such is "The Land o' the Leal," which is almost perfection. It was written originally with "John" instead of "Jean" as the name of the person apostrophised; and the verse beginning :—

"Sae dear that joy was bought, John,"

was added years afterwards owing to the religious convictions of the author. Such also are six beautiful songs dealing more or less with inanimate nature and the animal world, as well as with human life;—these are "The Auld House," "The Rowan Tree," "Bonnie ran the Burnie down," "The Mitherless Lammie," "The Robin's Nest," and "Caller Herrin'," the tune of which last represented the chime of the bells of the High Kirk of Edinburgh.

The Jacobite songs of Carolina Oliphant are likewise all but entirely her own. Some of these have exquisite pathos; witness the verses of "Will ye no come back again?"—

"Bonnie Charlie's now awa',
Safely owre the friendly main;
Mony a heart will break in twa
Should he ne'er come back again.

Will ye no come back again?
Will ye no come back again?
Better lo'ed ye canna be,
Will ye no come back again?
 •   •   •   •

"We watched thee in the gloamin' hour,
    We watched thee in the mornin' grey,
Tho' thirty thousand pounds they'd gie,
    Oh! there was nane that wad betray.

"Sweet's the laverock's note and lang,
    Lilting wildly up the glen;
But aye to me he sings ae sang,
    Will ye no come back again?"

The same may be said of the verses of "Charlie is my Darling:"—

"They've left their bonnie Hieland hills,
    Their wives and bairnies dear,
To draw the sword for Scotland's lord,
    The young Chevalier.
   •   •   •   •
"They proudly wore the milkwhite rose
    For him they lo'ed sae dear;
An' gave their sons to Charlie,
    The young Chevalier.

"Oh! there was mony a beatin' heart,
    An' mony a hope and fear,
An there was mony a prayer put up
    For the young Chevalier."

Truer fire can hardly burn in words than what is found in "Wha'll be King but Charlie?" and in the rampant triumph of "The Hundred Pipers;"—

"The Esk was swollen sae red and sae deep,
But shouther to shouther the brave lads keep;
Twa thousand swam ower to fell English ground,
An' danced themsel's dry to the pibroch's sound.
Dumbfounder'd the English saw—they saw,
Dumfounder'd they heard the blaw, the blaw!
Dumfounder'd they a' ran awa', awa',
From the hundred pipers an' a', an' a'."

"Ye'll mount, Gudeman" is more of a half humorous, half pathetic story sung in dialogue; and for the pathos see the gudewife's womanly regret over the severity of her cure:—

"The wily wife fleech'd, and the laird didna see
The smile on her cheek thro' the tear in her e'e;
Had I kent the gudeman wad hae had siccan pain,
The kettle for me sud hae coupet its lane."

Different fun altogether is the merry waggery in "The Laird o' Cockpen" (the title borrowed), "John Tod," "The Twa Doos," "Katie Reid's House" (still more of an adaptation), and in yet another adaptation, where sheer, exuberant nonsense prevails and tickles old and young alike, "Aiken Drum."

Among the sweetest of Lady Nairne's adaptations, and those which have the most of the woman in them, are "The Bonnie Brier-Bush" and "We're a' Noddin'." In "The Bonnie Brier-Bush," with a curiously life-like archness and tremulousness, the lassie doubts:—

"But were they a' true that were far awa'?
Oh! were they a' true that were far awa'?
They drew up wi' glaikit Englishers at Carlisle ha',
An' forgot auld frien's that were far awa'."

And stoutly and indignantly the laddie denies:—

"I ne'er lo'ed a dance but on Athole's green,
I ne'er lo'ed a lassie but my dorty Jean;
Sair, sair against my will did I bide sae lang awa',
An' my heart was aye in Athole's green at Carlisle ha'."

Then there comes over the couple in their blissful preoccupation the sorrowful remembrance of a lost cause and a nation's misfortunes:—

"The brier-bush was bonnie ance in our kailyard;
The brier-bush was bonnie ance in our kailyard;
A blast blew ower the hill, that gae Athole's flowers a chill,
And the bloom's blawn aff the bonnie bush in our kailyard.

In "We're a' Noddin'" with what delicate

distinctness the ancient figure by the ingle-neuk is painted :—

"Grannie nods i' the neuk and fends as she may,
An' brags that we'll ne'er be what she's been in her day,
Wow! but she was bonnie, and wow! but she was braw ;
An' she had routh o' wooers ance, I'se warrant, great and sma'."

How fond is the concluding conviction :—

"The bear's i' the brier, and the hay's i' the stack,
And a' will be richt again gin Jamie were come back."

The wisdom of the heart, which is conspicuous in Susanna Blamire's songs, finds clear expression in two of Lady Nairne's which are by no means her best artistically, but which breathe so happy a philosophy, so fine a moderation, that they deserve to live on the lips of her countrywomen. These are "The Bonniest Lass in a' the Warld" and "Saw ye ne'er a Lanely Lassie?" In the last Lady Nairne uses a very happy figure for the truth which she intends to teach :—

"Ilka state it has its blessings,
Peevish dinna pass them by,
But like choicest berries seek them,
Tho' amang the thorns they lie."

When later in life her mind had taken another bent, Lady Nairne's Jacobite prepossessions did not prevent her from writing on the opposite side of religion and politics. So we have her "Covenanter's Widow's Lament," her "Pentland Hills," and, it may be, also her "The Women are a' gane Wud." Save, however, in the last instance, either early influences were too strong for her, or the poetic vein was well-nigh exhausted, since the two former songs do not rank high among her lyrics.

There only remains for us to characterise the aged bereft woman's "Would you be Young again?" Sufficient to say that that final song is brokenly, touchingly eloquent, and lit up with heavenly radiance, worthy of all the picturesque and human-hearted songs which preceded it.

THE LAND O' THE LEAL.

I'm wearin' awa', John,
Like snaw-wreaths in thaw, John,
I'm wearin' awa'
    To the land o' the leal.

There's nae sorrow there, John,
There's neither cauld nor care, John,
The day is aye fair
   In the land o' the leal.

Our bonnie bairn's there, John,
She was baith gude and fair, John,
And, oh! we grudged her sair
   To the land o' the leal.

But sorrow's sel' wears past, John,
And joy is comin' fast, John,
The joy that's aye to last
   In the land o' the leal.

Sae dear 's that joy was bought, John,
Sae free the battle fought, John,
That sinfu' man e'er brought
   To the land o' the leal.

Oh! dry your glist'nin' e'e, John,
My soul langs to be free, John,
And angels beckon me
   To the land o' the leal.

Oh! haud ye leal an' true, John,
Your day it's wearin' thro', John,
And I'll welcome you
   To the land o' the leal.

Now fare ye weel, my ain John,
This warld's cares are vain, John,
We'll meet, and we'll be fain,
  In the land o' the leal.

CALLER HERRIN'.

Wha'll buy my caller herrin'?
They're bonnie fish and halesome farin';
Wha'll buy my caller herrin'
  New drawn frae the Forth?

When ye were sleepin' on your pillows,
Dreamed ye aught o' our puir fellows,
Darkling as they faced the billows,
A' to fill the woven willows?
  Buy my caller herrin',
  New drawn frae the Forth.

Wha'll buy my caller herrin'?
They're no brought here without brave darin';
Buy my caller herrin',
Haul'd thro' wind and rain.
  Wha'll buy my caller herrin'? &c.

Wha'll buy my caller herrin'?
Oh, ye may ca' them vulgar farin';
Wives and mithers, maist despairin',
Ca' them lives o' men.
    Wha'll buy my caller herrin'? &c.

When the creel o' herrin' passes,
Ladies, clad in silks and laces,
Gather in their braw pelisses,
Cast their heads, and screw their faces.
    Wha'll buy my caller herrin'? &c.

Caller herrin's no got lightlie,
Ye can trip the spring fu' tightlie;
Spite o' tauntin', flauntin', flingin',
Gow has set you a' a-singin'.
    Wha'll buy my caller herrin'? &c.

Neebour wives, now tent my tellin',
When the bonnie fish ye're sellin'
At ae word be in yer dealin'—
Truth will stand when a' thing's failin'.
  Wha'll buy my caller herrin'?
  They're bonnie fish and halesome farin';
  Wha'll buy my caller herrin'
    New drawn frae the Forth?

THE LAIRD O' COCKPEN.

The Laird o' Cockpen, he's proud an' he's great,
His mind is ta'en up wi' things o' the State;
He wanted a wife his braw house to keep,
But favour wi' wooin' was fashious to seek.

Down by the dyke-side a lady did dwell,
At his table-head he thought she'd look well—
McClish's ae daughter o' Claverse-ha'-Lee,
A penniless lass wi' a lang pedigree.

His wig was weel pouthered and as gude as new,
His waistcoat was white, his coat it was blue,
He put on a ring, a sword, and cock'd hat—
And wha could refuse the laird wi' a' that?

He took the grey mare, and rade cannily,
An' rapp'd at the gate o' Claverse-ha'-Lee:
"Gae tell Mistress Jean to come speedily ben,
She's wanted to speak to the Laird o' Cockpen."

Mistress Jean was makin' the elder-flower wine:
"An' what brings the laird at sic a like time?"
She put aff her apron, and on her silk gown,
Her mutch wi' red ribbons, an' gaed awa' down.

An' when she cam ben he bowed fu' low,
An' what was his errand he soon let her know;

Amazed was the laird when the lady said " Na,"
And wi' a laigh curtsie she turned awa'.

Dumfoundered was he, nae sigh did he gie,
He mounted his mare, and rade cannily,
An' aften he thought, as he gaed thro' the glen,
She's daft to refuse the Laird o' Cockpen.

THE AULD HOUSE.

Oh, the auld house, the auld house,
    What tho' the rooms were wee!
Oh, kind hearts were dwelling there,
    And bairnies fu' o' glee.
The wild rose and the jessamine
    Still hang upon the wa',
How mony cherished memories
    Do they, sweet flowers, reca'!

Oh, the auld laird, the auld laird!
    Sae canty, kind, and crouse,
How mony did he welcome to
    His ain wee dear auld house!

And the leddy too, sae genty,
　　There sheltered Scotland's heir,
And clipt a lock wi' her ain hand
　　Frae his lang yellow hair.

The mavis still doth sweetly sing,
　　The blue-bells sweetly blaw,
The bonny Earn's clear winding still,
　　But the auld house is awa'.
The auld house, the auld house,
　　Deserted tho' ye be,
There ne'er can be a new house
　　Will seem sae fair to me.

Still flourishing the auld pear-tree
　　The bairnies liked to see,
And oh, how often did they speir
　　When ripe they a' wad be!
The voices sweet, the wee bit feet
　　Aye rinnin' here and there,
The merry shout—oh! whiles we greet
　　To think we'll hear nae mair!

For they are a' wide scattered now,
　　Some to the Indies gane,
And ane, alas! to her lang hame;
　　Not here we'll meet again.

The kirkyaird, the kirkyaird !
  Wi' flowers o' every hue,
Sheltered by the holly's shade
  An' the dark sombre yew.

The setting sun, the setting sun,
  How glorious it gaed doon !
The cloudy splendour raised our hearts
  To cloudless skies aboon !
The auld dial, the auld dial !
  It tauld how time did pass ;
The wintry winds hae dung it doon,
  Now hid 'mang weeds and grass.

THE MITHERLESS LAMMIE.

The mitherless lammie ne'er missed its ain mammie,
  We tentit it kindly by nicht and by day ;
The bairnies made game o't, it had a blythe hame o't,
  Its food was the gowan, wi' dew-drops o' May.
Without tie or fetter, it couldna been better,
  But it wad gae witless the wide warld to see ;
The foe that it feared not, it saw not, it heard not,
  Was watching its wanderings frae Bonnington Lea.

Oh what then befel it, 'twere waefu' to tell it,
   Tod Lowrie kens best, wi' his lang head sae sly ;
He met the pet lammie, that wanted its mammie,
   And left its kind hame the wide warld to try.
We missed it at day dawin', we missed it at night fa'in,
   Its wee shed is tenantless under the tree ;
A e nicht i' the gloamin', it wad gae a roamin',
   'Twill frolic nae mair upon Bonnington Lea.

KIND ROBIN LO'ES ME.

Robin is my ain gudeman,
Now match him, carlins, gin ye can,
For ilk ane whitest thinks her swan,
   But kind Robin lo'es me.
To mak my boast I'll e'en be bauld,
For Robin lo'ed me young and auld,
In simmer's heat and winter's cauld,
   My kind Robin lo'es me.

Robin he comes hame at e'en
Wi' pleasure glancin' in his een ;
He tells me a' he's heard and seen,
   And syne how he lo'es me.

There's some hae land and some hae gowd,
And mair wad hae them gin they could,
But a' I wish o' warld's gude
   Is Robin aye to lo'e me.

THE ROWAN TREE.

Oh, Rowan tree! oh, Rowan tree! thou'lt aye be dear to me,
Entwined thou art wi' mony ties o' hame and infancy;
Thy leaves were aye the first o' spring, thy flowers the simmer's pride;
There wasna sic a bonny tree in a' the country side.
                Oh! Rowan tree.

How fair wert thou in simmer time, wi' a' thy clusters white,
How rich and gay thy autumn dress, wi' berries red and bright;
On thy fair stem were mony names, which now nae mair I see,
But they're engraven on my heart—forgot they ne'er can be!
                Oh! Rowan tree.

We sat aneath thy spreading shade, the bairnies round
    thee ran,
They pu'd thy bonny berries red, and necklaces they
    strang ;
My mother! oh ! I see her still, she smiled our sports to see,
Wi' little Jeanie on her lap, an' Jamie at her knee !
                      Oh ! Rowan tree.

Oh ! there arose my father's prayer, in holy evening's
    calm,
How sweet was then my mother's voice in the Martyrs'
    psalm ;
Now a' are gane ! we meet nae mair aneath the Rowan
    tree,
But hallowed thoughts around thee twine o' hame and
    infancy.
                      Oh ! Rowan tree.

AIKIN DRUM.

There lived a man in our toun,
  In our toun, in our toun,
There lived a man in our toun
    And they ca'd him Aikin Drum.
And he wad be a soger, a soger, a soger,
    And he wad be a soger,
And they ca'd him Aikin Drum.

And his coat was o' the gude saut meat,
The gude saut meat, the gude saut meat,
And a waistcoat o' the haggis-bag
    Aye wore Aikin Drum.
O' the gude lang kail and the Athole brose,
Aye they made his trews and hose ;
And he luiket weel, as ye may suppose,
    And his name was Aikin Drum.

And his bonnet was made o' pie crust,
O' pie crust, o' pie crust,
And his bonnet was made o' pie crust,
    Built baith thick an' soun'.
And he played upon a razor,
A razor, a razor,
And he played upon a razor,
    And whiles upon the kame.

And he lo'ed weel the crappit heads,
The crappit heads, and singet heads,
And he lo'ed weel the crappit heads
    And singet heads an' a';
And he lo'ed weel the ait cake,
The ait cake, the ait cake,
And he lo'ed weel the ait cake,
    And scones and bannocks a'.

But wae's me! he turned soger,
A soger, a soger,
But wae's me! he turned soger,
And he was marched awa'.
'Bout him the carles were gabbin',
For him the laddies sabbin',
And a' the lassies greetin',
For Aikin Drum's awa'.

WHA'LL BE KING BUT CHARLIE?

The news frae Moidart cam' yestreen
Will soon gar mony ferlie;
For ships o' war hae just come in
And landit Royal Charlie.

Come thro' the heather, around him gather,
Ye're a' the welcomer early;
Around him cling wi' a' your kin;
For wha'll be king but Charlie?
Come thro' the heather, around him gather,
Come Ronald, come Donald, come a' thegither,
And crown your rightfu', lawfu' king!
For wha'll be king but Charlie?

The Hieland clans, wi' sword in hand,
　　Frae John o' Groat's to Airlie,
Hae to a man declared to stand
　　Or fa' wi' Royal Charlie.
　　　　　　Come thro' the heather, &c.

The Lowlands a', baith great an' sma',
　　Wi' mony a lord and laird, hae
Declared for Scotia's king an' law,
　　An' speir ye wha but Charlie.
　　　　　　Come thro' the heather, &c.

There's ne'er a lass in a' the lan'
　　But vows baith late an' early,
She'll ne'er to man gie heart nor han'
　　Wha wadna fecht for Charlie.
　　　　　　Come thro' the heather, &c.

Then here's a health to Charlie's cause,
　　And be't complete an' early;
His very name our heart's blood warms;
　　To arms for Royal Charlie!
　　　　　　Come thro' the heather, &c.

CHARLIE IS MY DARLING.

'Twas on a Monday morning
  Right early in the year,
When Charlie came to our toun,
  The Young Chevalier.
    Oh, Charlie is my darling,
      My darling, my darling,
    Oh, Charlie is my darling,
      The Young Chevalier.

As he cam' marching up the street,
  The pipes played loud and clear,
And a' the folk cam' runnin' out
  To meet the Chevalier.
    Oh, Charlie is my darling, &c.

Wi' Hieland bonnets on their heads,
  And claymores bright and clear;
They cam' to fight for Scotland's right,
  And the Young Chevalier.
    Oh, Charlie is my darling, &c.

They've left their bonnie Hieland hills,
  Their wives and bairnies dear,
To draw the sword for Scotland's lord,
  The Young Chevalier.
    Oh, Charlie is my darling, &c.

Oh, there were mony beatin' hearts,
And mony a hope and fear;
And mony were the prayers put up
For the Young Chevalier.
   Oh, Charlie is my darling, &c.

HE'S OWER THE HILLS THAT I LO'E WEEL.

He's ower the hills that I lo'e weel,
He's ower the hills we daurna name;
He's ower the hills ayont Dumblane,
Wha soon will get his welcome hame.
   He's ower the hills, &c.

My father's gane to fecht for him,
My brithers winna bide at hame;
My mither greets and prays for them,
And 'deed she thinks they're no to blame.
   He's ower the hills, &c.

The Whigs may scoff, the Whigs may jeer,
But ah! that love maun be sincere
Which still keeps true whate'er betide,
An' for his sake leaves a' beside.
   He's ower the hills, &c.

His right these hills, his right these plains ;
O'er Hieland hearts secure he reigns ;
What lads e'er did our lads will do ;
Were I a laddie, I'd follow him too.
He's ower the hills, &c.

Sae noble a look, sae princely an air,
Sae gallant an' bold, sae young an' sae fair ;
Oh ! did ye but see him, ye'd do as we've done ;
Hear him but ance, to his standard you'll run.
He's ower the hills, &c.

JOHN TOD.

He's a terrible man, John Tod, John Tod,
  He's a terrible man, John Tod.
He scolds in the house, he scolds at the door,
He scolds on the verra high road, John Tod,
  He scolds on the verra high road.

The weans a' fear John Tod, John Tod,
  The weans a' fear John Tod ;
When he's passing by, the mithers will cry,
" Here's an ill wean, John Tod, John Tod,
  Here's an ill wean, John Tod."

The callants a' fear John Tod, John Tod,
   The callants a' fear John Tod.
If they steal but a neep, the laddie he'll whip,
And it's unco weel done o' John Tod, John Tod,
   It's unco' weel done o' John Tod.

An' saw ye na wee John Tod, John Tod,
   O saw ye na wee John Tod ;
His bannet was blue, his shoon maistly new,
And weel does he keep the kirk road, John Tod,
   O weel does he keep the kirk road.

How is he fendin', John Tod, John Tod?
   How is he wendin', John Tod?
He's scourin' the land wi' his rung in his hand,
And the French wadna frighten John Tod, John
     Tod,
   And the French wadna frighten John Tod.

Ye're sun-brunt and battered, John Tod, John Tod,
   Ye're tautit and tattered, John Tod ;
Wi' your auld strippit coul, ye luik maist like a fule,
But there's nouse i' the lining, John Tod, John Tod,
   But there's nouse i' the lining, John Tod.

He's weel respeckit, John Tod, John Tod,
   He's weel respeckit, John Tod ;

He's a terrible man, but we'd a' gae wrang
If e'er he sud leave us, John Tod, John Tod,
If e'er he sud leave us, John Tod.

REST IS NOT HERE.

What's this vain world to me?—
  Rest is not here;
False are the smiles I see,
  The mirth I hear.
Where is youth's joyful glee?
Where all once dear to me?
Gone as the shadows flee—
  Rest is not here.

Why did the morning shine
  Blithely and fair?
Why did those tints so fine
  Vanish in air?
Does not the vision say,
Faint, lingering heart, away;
Why in this desert stay?
  Dark land of care!

Where souls angelic soar,
   Thither repair ;
Let this vain world no more
   Lull and ensnare.
That heaven I love so well,
Still in my heart shall dwell ;*
All things around me tell
   Rest is found there.

WOULD YOU BE YOUNG AGAIN?

Would you be young again?
   So would not I;
One tear to memory given,
   Onward I'd hie.
Life's dark flood forded o'er,
All but at rest on shore,
Say, would you plunge once more,
   With home so nigh?

If you might, would you now
   Retrace your way?
Wander through thorny wilds,
   Faint and astray?

* Compare last verse of " Robin Adair."

Night's gloomy watches fled,
Morning all beaming red,
Hope's smiles around us shed,
　Heavenward—away.

Where are they gone, of yore
　My best delight?
Dear and more dear, tho' now
　Hidden from sight.
Where they rejoice to be,
There is the land for me;
Fly, time! fly speedily;
　Come, life and light.

JOANNA BAILLIE.

1762—1851.

IN the autumn of 1762 a Scotch minister's family made a quiet "flitting" from the parish of Shotts to the neighbouring parish of Bothwell, in Lanarkshire. Besides the minister's books and his lady's work-table, there was a cradle, which had been already thrice filled; and immediately on the family's arrival in the cold quarters of a new home, it was prematurely replenished by a delicate baby girl, whose twin sister died at her birth. That tiny half-blighted bud of a child, named after her uncle, Dr. John Hunter, the great anatomist, developed into an ardent, aspiring, largely endowed Scotchwoman. She was the most sensible of wilful geniuses; the most retiring of "wise" women; the most maidenly of experienced elderly ladies; the most tenderly attached of daughters and sisters; one of the meekest and most modest of Christians. Joanna Baillie's was a noble soul. She had a great man's grand guilelessness, rather than a woman's minute and subtle powers of sympathy; a man's shy but unstinted kindness and forbearance rather than a woman's eager but measured cordiality and softness; a man's modesty in full combination with a woman's delicacy; and, as if to prove her sex beyond mistake, she had, after all, more than the usual share of a woman's tenacity and headstrongness, when the fit was upon her. It is not so much with Joanna Baillie, the well-known author of the "Plays of the Passions," that we have to do here, as with Joanna Baillie, the singer of "Wooed and Married and a'" and "'Saw ye Johnnie comin,' quo she?"—the Joanna Baillie who, quitting Scotland a girl, and not returning till she was a middle-aged woman, grown famous in the interval, came back speaking broader Scotch than when she left.

Another explanation may be needed. Unless destroyed for special reasons, there must exist ample materials for a full and interesting life of one of the first and best of English literary women; but, as these materials have not been given to the world, a sketch of Joanna Baillie is all that can be drawn here. At least this sketch will not be slighter than many of the previous sketches, which have been made from formal narratives and meagre traditions.

Joanna Baillie's father and mother had both good Scotch blood in their veins. He was come of Baillies "sib" to the Baillies of Lamington and Jerviswoode. She was a Hunter of Hunterston. He was a learned and laborious man. She was a daughter in an original and clever family, and had herself such an appreciation of what was original in human nature, as to render her a good teller of a story. Both father and mother, too, were rarely high-principled; and, in spite of his warm affections and her latent faculties of humour and pathos, they were alike strongly tinged with the strict, somewhat stern, reserve of the old Scotch character.

Agnes Baillie (Joanna's sister) told Lucy Aikin that, though her father had sucked the poison from a bite which she had received from a dog believed to be mad, he had never kissed her in his life. Joanna herself spoke to the same friend of her unsatisfied yearning for caresses when a child, and of her mother's simply chiding her when she ventured to clasp that mother's knees; "but," Joanna added, with perfect comprehension, "I know she liked it."

And Joanna had playmates, while the austere and hardy life at the manse of Bothwell was suffered to include much out-of-door freedom and active sport. Her sister Agnes's tender but much less powerful fancy, in its early fondness for stories of every description, stimulated Joanna to surmount the first Hill Difficulty of her letters; and her brother Matthew, most upright, skilful, and kindly of physicians, as well as most trusty and faithful of kinsmen, was the comrade of Joanna's youth, before he followed in the steps of his uncles, the great anatomists, and lived to be the fashionable and court doctor of the West-end of London.

The village of Bothwell, where Dr. James Baillie's kirk and manse were situated, possessed many advantages. It was where "Clyde's banks are bonnie," in the fruit lands of the middle ward of Lanarkshire, and where there is a strath of waving verdure at all seasons. In May and June it is one great white and pink flush of orchard blossoms. In August and September boughs bend richly under purple plums, scarlet streaked apples, and mottled olive and russet pears. Close by are the fragments of the great castle-keep of the Douglasses, one of the most stately ruins of Scotland. In the kirk of Bothwell, where Joanna's father preached, the grim Earl of Angus's hard-featured, sour-spirited daughter, Marjory Douglas, was wedded on an "ill-day" to poor wild David of Rothesay, already troth-plighted to Elizabeth Dunbar. At a mile's distance from Bothwell village stands Bothwell Brig, where, on another and still more memorable day, Monmouth, Dalzell, and Claverse broke and scattered the Covenanters, who, driven to desperation by the persecutions after the murder of Archbishop Sharpe, had made head at Drumclog. All around, among waving trees or out on moors, are Bothwell Haugh, the Cartlane Crags, the Dog of Biggar, Loudon, Tinto.

The Baillies were not likely to take less interest in some of these localities that, through their ancestors of Lamington, they claimed descent from the only daughter of Wallace; while with their ancient kinsmen of Jerviswoode they had been in the thick of the troubles of the Kirk. But other legends, besides those of tolerably well authenticated history, lurked in each drearier spot of that country. Vague tales of the foul fiend himself started up in the desolation of a peat bog, or the horror of a gruesome cavern. The familiar spirit of Michael Scott was said to have come face to face with the frenzied Covenanters, — the warlock cleaving the defile of the Sandy Hill Nick, and throwing down the stones of the Yelpin Craigs. Or more awful still, there were legends of grey "bogles" and sheeted ghosts haunting the cairns of murdered men, women, and bairns, down among the dark shores of Blantyre, or in the middle of the waste of "the long whang" of Carnwath Muir. These were the common chronicles and fire-side lore of the country people of the day. As a stirring, inquisitive child, Joanna Baillie had a good source from which she could derive such knowledge, and form a familiar acquaintance betimes with many-sided humanity. The kitchen of the country manse was then the free resort and resting-place of privileged beggars, old soldiers and sailors, and humble travellers of every description. The settle in the chimney, and the "bink" in the "hallan," were rarely empty, as backwards and forwards trotted the little maid herself, making believe to dispense the doles of bannocks and cheese, and the cogs of brose and kale. All the while she was gathering scraps of racy conversation into wide-open little pitchers of ears, and photographing still more accurately in clear fresh mirrors of eyes the quaintly-expressive faces and figures.

In remote years Joanna painted a very pleasant picture of her own and her sister's childhood at Bothwell :—

> "Two tiny imps, who scarcely stooped to gather
> The slender hare-bell or the purple heather,
> No taller than the foxglove's spiky stem,
> That dew of morning studs with silvery gem.
> Then every butterfly that crossed our view
> With joyful shout was greeted as it flew;
> And moth, and ladybird, and beetle bright
> In shiny gold were each a wondrous sight.
> Then as we paddled bare-foot, side by side,
> Among the sunny shallows of the Clyde,
> Minnows and spotted par with twinkling fin,
> Swimming in mazy rings the pool within,
> A thrill of gladness through our bosoms sent,
> Seen in the power of early wonderment."

All that Joanna learnt directly at Bothwell was in early childhood. She was not more than six years old when her father exchanged the kirk of Bothwell for that of Hamilton, likewise in the fruit lands. But Hamilton was a town of six thousand inhabitants, clustering round the ducal palace and park of the Hamiltons. Here Joanna found herself one of a community which numbered scores of young people of her own age and degree. So well did she like it, that she was the leader in every romping game and frolic, — an adept at out-of-door sports, whether swinging, skipping, or climbing. She was celebrated for the fearlessness with which she ran along the parapets of bridges and on the tops of walls, and scampered heedlessly on any pony she could find. She had the misfortune to cause the fracture of her brother's arm, by inducing him to ride double with her on another horse than Pegasus. The horse, not approving of a pair of riders, threw the one who had the worse seat. "Look at Miss Jack!" a farmer once commented, lost in admiration of the girl's "noble horsemanship," as she proceeded in advance of the party which she accompanied on a country excursion; "she sits her horse as if it was a bit of herself."

Joanna Baillie was born a leader. She was physically very courageous; a fact which she probably owed in part to her peculiarly healthy training. She knew how priceless were the privileges she had enjoyed in this respect. In advanced life she loved to dwell on her early unchecked rambles over heaths compared to which Hampstead was a common; on her endless "paidling" in innumerable burns, tributaries of the Clyde; and on the intimate terms on which these habits had put her with great Nature. She was wont to regret wistfully that she could no longer "pad" barefooted on the grass or "plowter" in the water. And she would eagerly recommend to dainty and horrified English matrons the entire wholesomeness and happiness of letting their petted children run barefooted in summer.

Whatever more valuable acquisitions Joanna made in these young days, she was singularly deficient in learning—as the term is generally understood. Little Fanny Burney was erudite compared to Joanna Baillie, notwithstanding that Fanny declined dull printed books, and preferred to read on the animated tables of flesh which were presented to her in the faces of the clever men and women thronging her father's house. "At nine I could not read plainly," Joanna Baillie told

Lucy Aikin. "At nine, Joanna?" her sister Agnes called her back. "You could not read well at eleven."

The worthy minister took the stout little ignoramus in hand along with his breakfast. She spoilt the flavour of his trout and cake and black pudding by crying throughout each lesson. Yet, bookish as Dr. Baillie was, his own tastes did not blind him to Joanna's natural capabilities. Nay, paternal affection might help him to resist prejudice. Did not the natural history of the fruit lands remind him that the choice standard trees were those of slow, gradual growth? Certainly he signalised his penetration by maintaining Joanna's quickness and correctness of observation. "The child is not stupid in other things than books. Joanna will be 'the flower o' the flock' yet." "Honest Mat" got Latin to render into English verses at his school, and found himself unequal to the task. "Joanna will do it," said the father; and Joanna did it, and this was her first triumph in verse. And then her handiness with the needle (hear it all those who must needs believe an authoress "handless") is said to have been remarkable.

However, it was thought that a change was called for, in order to conquer Joanna's repugnance to sedentary studies, and her passion for open-air pursuits and boyish pranks. At ten years of age she was accordingly sent, along with her elder sister, to Miss Macdonald's boarding-school, in the heart of the city of Glasgow. To be sure, boarding-schools at that time were more schools of manners than of intellectual knowledge. Among the few branches taught in them, the sewing of satin pieces and the art of sitting with straight backs took a prominent place. But there is this to be said. Elaborate embroidery on satin and the keeping of the restless young body under entire control, drew forth the primary elements of attention and application about as well as any other earnest effort.

Joanna learned to read perfectly at the Glasgow boarding-school, as doubtless she also learned more or less serviceable writing and arithmetic, and correct or incorrect notions in geography and history. If she did not learn much else beyond singing a little to the guitar, and making a few promising attempts at drawing and dancing, still the school did its part.

But the study for which she showed a particular inclination was mathematics—a fact which is not only characteristic of the clear-headed girl, it is also evidence of the liberal possibilities of these decried old schools. Of her own free will and entirely unassisted, she mastered a considerable portion of Euclid. But Joanna was never what might be called a deeply-read woman. The friend of her middle age, Lucy Aikin—a fair classical scholar and an accomplished modern linguist—far exceeded Joanna in these respects. Yet, though Lucy Aikin joined to such acquirements fine penetration, good judgment, and correct taste, she stood as far behind Joanna Baillie in natural ability as Joanna surpassed her in learning, and Lucy Aikin herself would have been the first to admit it.

Pricked on by the demands, and the power of supplying the demands, of a large girl audience at school, Joanna's hereditary gift of story-telling, by which she could excite laughter or tears, grew and grew until at length she found herself the chief figure in something like private theatricals. In connection with these chamber dramas Joanna was play-writer, playwright, player, stage-dresser, and scene-shifter in one. In this foreshadowing of her future career, she is said to have strongly displayed an eye for effect, which failed her in the great efforts of later life.

Let us conjure up, if we can, the old Glasgow boarding-school, with its small rooms and dim tallow candles. There stand the host of eager girls in their short-waisted, short-sleeved gowns and mittens, absorbed in the common levy of buckles, brooches, necklaces, plaids, scarfs, breast-knots, and the Highland bonnets which are still worn by girls. The acknowledged mistress of the ceremonies and games, and the "first lady" of the troop, is the undersized girl with marked features and grey eyes, who is to become the friend of Scott and Channing. Down on the scene Miss Macdonald and her governess look for a moment, from the elevation of their huge toupees and barricades of ruffles. They dismiss authoritatively the excited rabble, and retire to their cosy supper, where they admit in confidence to each other the mother-wit of Miss Jack Baillie, who has yet got a bad memory for facts of consequence outside of her "fulè" stories, and her "droll swatches" of this man and that woman.

Joanna Baillie returned to Hamilton with the dignity of a finished young lady; but she did not long remain one of the belles of the country town. She was not more than fifteen when her father was appointed to a professorship in Glasgow University. The Baillies removed to the city, and were established within the precincts of the College in the High Street. Glasgow was then in a transition state like other towns. The Virginian merchants, ruined by the American war, had first shown diminished heads and then as a class disappeared. A few of their descendants and a sprinkling of the local gentry still made head against new trades and new-comers, and continued to occupy houses in the Saltmarket and the Briggate, with armorial bearings above the doors. The grand cathedral alone resisted all influences of time and men, whether dedicated to St. Mungo or to St. Mungo's Master, whether divided into the chancel, the crypt, and the dripping aisle, or into the High Kirk and the Laigh Kirk.

The learned atmosphere of the college had its influence on Joanna in spite of her old quarrels with learning. She was innocently proud to be a denizen of the city. The imposing stretch of civilisation expressed in the Trongate, with the sobering, elevating glory of the cathedral, were not without their effect upon her. It is possible that Miss Mally Campbell was another instrument in shaping Joanna's course. Miss Mally was not only one of the most intellectual women of her day, but she held as powerful sway over old Glasgow College society as Miss Jacky Murray, Lord Mansfield's sister, had previously maintained over the early Edinburgh assemblies. We are told that Joanna was considered a well-bred, clever girl for the period and the position—so much so as to "cast an awe" over her companions. Indeed, it is hard to conceive Joanna as having ever been boisterous even in her childish escapades. In her simplicity she was one of the most perfect of gentlewomen, and one of the most maidenly of shrewd and honest-spoken women. Already she was fond of argument, and obstinate, if not unreasonable, when unconvinced.

If Joanna cherished dreams of living long years in Glasgow College, of seeing the ships advance higher and higher up the brimming Clyde, and of marrying at last some young professor bold enough to attempt clipping the wings already evincing a tendency to soar, all these fair prospects were suddenly brought to an end. Her father died in middle life, two years after his settlement in the University. She was then in her seventeenth year. In her extreme age, when addressing some lines to an infant James Baillie, she thus recalls his great-grandfather's worth :—

> "Thou wear'st his name who, in his stinted span
> Of human life, a generous, useful man,
> Did well the pastor's honour'd task perform.
> The toilsome way, the winter's beating storm,

Ne'er kept him from the peasant's distant cot,
Where want and suffering were the inmate's lot;
Who look'd for comfort in his friendly face,
As by the sick-bed's side he took his place.
A peace-maker in each divided home,
To him all strife-perplex'd folk would come.
In after years, how earnestly he strove
In sacred lore his students to improve ;
As they met round the academic chair,
Each felt a zealous friend address'd him there.
He was thy grandsire's sire, who in his day,
That, many years gone by, hath passed away,
On human gratitude had many claims.
Be thou as good a man, my little James."

Save for the widow's slender annuity, Dr. Baillie's family were dependent on Joanna's uncles. According to their arrangement, Mrs. Baillie at once left Glasgow, and went to Dr. William Hunter's small estate and house of Long Calderwood, in the Middle Ward of Lanarkshire. There she spent the first portion of her widowhood in great seclusion. Joanna might have gained some city tastes, but she certainly had not lost her country predilections. Recovering from the shock which had shaken the family and altered the tenor of their life, she fell back on her old delight of long walks and scrambles by the river Calder. But the comparative loneliness of Long Calderwood, felt all the more now that the young people had enjoyed something of a more animated and exciting life, drove Joanna to books as a resource. Though she never became a great reader, she began to know almost by heart, Shakspeare and Milton, Dryden and Pope. Poetry, especially dramatic declamatory poetry, captivated her strong mind.

The brothers Hunter exercised a greater power over the fortunes of the Baillies than even rich uncles are in the habit of exercising. Dr. John Hunter was married, and had a family; but Dr. William, the elder brother, was a bachelor, and soon adopted Matthew Baillie as his successor. Dr. William Hunter accordingly sent Matthew to keep his terms at Balliol College, Oxford. The country house in the moors of Lanarkshire was thus rendered quieter and more monotonous still by the absence of the only son. The retirement pressed a little even on the much-enduring women, especially when their season of mourning wore past. In the year 1783, when Joanna was twenty-one years of age, Mrs. Baillie and her daughters went to Glasgow, and spent the winter there; the young girls renewing their old acquaintanceships and friendships formed at Miss Macdonald's school.

At this time Joanna appeared to her companions a capable young woman, with much decision of character, like her mother. She was shy amongst strangers, but sufficiently frank to her friends; and in the midst of her seriousness, she was the merriest soul when the fit took her. She had quietly written some clever Scotch songs, most of them adaptations from old ditties. These were already sung with glee round many a rustic hearth, and at many a homely supper-table. They were such songs as would doubtless have preserved the whisper of the singer's name in the Middle Ward if she had become one of its douce and careful matrons, long after she was taken up with weightier duties, and tempted to disown such trifles.

Joanna was not handsome. In her graceful and kindly lines to her sister Agnes, on her birthday, Joanna reminds her sister of her early superiority in look and manner:—

> "Thy fairer face and sprightlier courtesy
> (A truth that from my youthful vanity
> Lay not concealed) did for the sisters twain,
> Where'er we went, the greater favour gain."

Joanna was below the middle height, and had the large, statuesque features which suit better with a stately figure. Years lent these features dignity rather than robbed them of grace. There is no word of her youthful bloom. She wore her hair for many years simply divided and braided across her forehead; but the hair must have grown low on it from the first, and, whether in a crop, or in braids, must have nearly concealed the expansive brow, which thus lent no relief to the dark gauntness of the face. Her grey eyes were good and well opened, but grave, though humour could dance in them. The brows were firmly arched. Her mouth was wide, and expressed benevolence. Her chin was clearly moulded, and slightly projecting.

Joanna's was at this time a pent-up face, like the character of which it was the index.

The year 1784 saw another phase of the Baillies' history. Dr. William Hunter died, and left to his nephew, Matthew Baillie, the estate of Long Calderwood, as well as his house in London. He had added to his London house an anatomical theatre, lecture-room, and museum, but the valuable contents of the latter were to be transferred to Glasgow College at the end of thirty years. By the last bequest he disinherited his brother John, whose marriage had displeased him. Matthew Baillie was then a young man, unknown and untried, just entering on the struggle of his profession. His mother and sisters, to whom he was warmly attached, were not lavishly provided for, though not dependent upon him. He did not hesitate, however, but at once gave up the estate of Long Calderwood to Dr. John Hunter, who had been its presumptive heir, preferring to trust to his own ability and industry. Many men would call such a deed strained and far-fetched in a novel; but Matthew Baillie did it. Not only so,

He and his mother and sisters seem to have regarded it as the simplest act in the world—the only one, in fact, that was left him to do. In place of keeping Long Calderwood, and settling his mother and sisters in it, Matthew Baillie made over the house and property to his surviving uncle, and took his family up to London in that year, 1784, to share with him his fortunes in the middle of the wilderness of stone and lime of Windmill Street.

To these self-contained, gently-born Scotchwomen, accustomed to the fresh air of the country, the change was so great and so trying, as to prove an exile in which they were likely to feel lonelier and more isolated than they had ever felt among the moors of Lanarkshire. They had with them the affectionate son and brother, now risen to be the head of the house; but he was all day abroad, busy in the lecture-rooms, or the hospitals, or at the sickbeds of his first patients. Besides all this, he was unlike his family, tolerant as he might be of their prejudices. He had been in England from boyhood: his very dialect was softened. English ways were natural to him, and he had formed many associations and ties which were strange to them.

It was a mercy that the house in Windmill Street was a large one, so that Joanna had ample opportunities for space and solitude. When her body was cramped with the confinement and with her avoidance of the crowded, glaring city streets, and when the weary longing for the wild braes of the Calder was upon her, she could retreat to unoccupied halls, as the anatomical theatre and museum might appear to her. She could find relief in promenading past skeletons and mummies, grinning and glowering at her in the twilight, and in gazing idly upon pictures of nature and portraits of great men; or in turning over cases of coins, of curious Indian workmanship, such as must have caught her lively fancy. Another resource for Joanna was that her uncle and name-father, Dr. John Hunter (alienation from whom was prevented by Matthew Baillie's prompt justice) had married a Scotchwoman, a sister of Sir Everard Home. Mrs. John Hunter was an elegant and accom-

plished woman, and was the centre of a polished
and brilliant circle, in which the original genius
of her husband shone like a rough diamond.
She was the author of some lyrics, which were
much admired by her own set in that day; and
some of them, like the "Indian Chief's Death
Song," may well be admired in any day. Her
songs were contributed to "Scotch Miscellanies
of Music," and one of them in particular was
set to music by Haydn. This song, "My mother
bids me bind my hair," has such a charm of
simplicity,—highly artificial indeed, but the perfection of art personates artlessness,—and is so
wedded to its exquisite air, that there is little
chance of its being forgotten.

 Joanna Baillie, though she far surpassed her
aunt in breadth and depth of intellect, had yet
a good deal in common with her, and could be
improved by Mrs. Hunter's culture. At her
house Joanna must have met society calculated
to interest her and to excite her dormant powers.
By some of the visitors there, Joanna was no
doubt looked upon as a stiff, solemn Scotch
girl, uncouth and raw-boned in mind, if *petite*

and slight in person, who, only through the good offices of her beautiful and tasteful aunt, was dressed in becoming clothing.

Whether it was the effect of

"The expressive glow of woman's noon,"

or of the compulsory sedentariness of a city life, in the year 1790, when she was in her twenty-ninth year, Joanna composed and published (with genuine Scotch caution—anonymously) a volume of miscellaneous poems. The book made little impression, as might well be the case when it afforded so slight an indication of the genius of its writer. Joanna's whole history is the very opposite of rank growth. It is rather the slow development and gradual ripening of strong, rich fibre. One generously discriminating critic who praised the faithful descriptions of nature in the book, comforted Joanna a little for the silence and indifference of the mass both of censors and readers. She was saved from the mortifying persuasion that she had utterly miscalculated what she could do.

One broodingly hot summer afternoon of this

year Joanna sat, in phlegmatic mood, sewing beside her mother in the "gloomy" house, apparently thinking of nothing except whether Matthew would come home to drink a cup of the tea which Agnes was infusing, or whether he would go round by the Denmans'—a house that had lately offered a potent attraction to him. But in reality Joanna's mind was dwelling on nothing so purely domestic. She was still smarting under her disappointment, and pondering the cause of her failure.

All at once there flashed upon her the idea that she had made a mistake, and that dramatic composition was the channel into which her genius should flow. Joanna Baillie was at once the least unwavering and the least rash of women. She went to her room that very afternoon, and projected a tragedy called *Arnold*. She worked at it unfalteringly for three months, and finished it; but it never saw the light. It was not till after eight years— those momentous eight years when many governments and many minds were heaving in the great moral and social earthquake—that she published the first volume of the "Plays of the Passions." Neither within that period nor at any future time did she swerve from the faith which she had reached as at a bound, that her talent was not only dramatic, but that her conception of the drama was the true conception.

In the following year, 1791, the family home in Windmill Street was broken up by the marriage of Matthew Baillie to Sophia Denman, daughter of Dr. Denman and sister of the future Lord Chief Justice of the Queen's Bench. The shady house in the dark street was left to the sunshine of young wedded love. Joanna gives an idealised portrait of her sister-in-law in birthday verses, addressed to Mrs. Baillie, in 1813:—

> "A judgment clear, a pensive mind,
> With feelings tender and refined;
> A generous heart in kindness glowing,
> An open hand, on all bestowing;
> A temper sweet, and calm, and even,
> Through petty provocations given.
> A soul benign, whose cheerful leisure
> Considers still of others' pleasure;
> Or in its lonely, graver mood,
> Considers still of others' good.

> And joined to these, the vision'd eye
> And tuneful ear of poesy.
> Blest wight, in whom these gifts combine,
> Our dear Sophia, sister mine.
> * * * *
> Through years unmarked by woe or pain,
> Oft may this day return again;
> Blessed by him whose rough career
> Of toil and care thy love doth cheer;
> Whose manly worth by heaven was fated
> To be through life thus fitly mated."

It is the likeness of a gentle, delicate-minded lady, who was very happily circumstanced throughout her whole life—in her early nurture, in her husband, in her very sister-in-law, whose nature was so daring in its self-sufficing reticence and fearless firmness. For, though Joanna could be vehement, impatient, hard, and stubborn to characters in full contention with her, there were no limits to her forbearance and generosity in dealing with the pacific and the unpretending, not to say the weak. While she was far too guileless to object to independence of opinion or action, like a man she loved to protect, encourage, and guide; and it ought in fairness to be recorded that, like a man, she could also magnanimously forego her pledged hostility and forget her registered resentment. Joanna's relations with her sister-in-law were, from first to last, very happy ones. Her affection for her brother's two children, and in the course of years for their children, was remarkable even in a woman who was naturally fond of both children and animals. Indeed, opposed as the description may be to the popular notion of a tragic muse, Joanna was, to abuse a systematically abused English word, always a very "comfortable" daughter, sister, aunt, and grand-aunt.

Mrs. Baillie and her daughters tried various situations before they fixed upon their dwelling-place—the dwelling-place that was to last to the daughter for well-nigh half a century. They removed to Colchester for several years; but the attraction of London was too strong for them. While the family were still flitting here and there, Joanna brought out in 1798, when in her thirty-seventh year, the first volume of her "Plays of the Passions." It contained *Basil*, a tragedy on love; a comedy on the same passion; and *De Mont-*

fort, a tragedy on hatred. Her theory included a high moral aim, the careful and finished delineation of character, and the growth and development of a master-passion with its inner spring and motive power.

She boldly and decidedly stated in her introduction that this theory was the higher utterance of the drama, though the neglected one; and, consistently with this opinion, she dogmatically undervalued circumstance and incident when used as opposing sources of interest.

This volume was also given to the world anonymously. In the life of Joanna Baillie, which is prefixed to the collected edition of her works, it is stated that "the author was sought for with avidity among the most gifted personages of the day." This gives the impression that the plays had created an immediate and unusual sensation. But according to Mary Berry's report very little account of the volume was made by her set the first winter, although she herself showed discrimination in readily appreciating the plays, and in crying them up everywhere. A copy had been sent to her from the author (possibly at Mrs. John Hunter's suggestion), and Miss Berry could not conjecture who had paid her the compliment. In March, 1799, Mary writes of the author as still undiscovered, and as having "quietly waited a whole twelvemonth for the impression the volume had at last made on an obdurate public," after Sir George Beaumont and Fox were in raptures, and Mrs. Siddons was speaking of the plays with surprise and delight.

Whether the Strawberry-Hill coterie, whose head, Horace Walpole, had closed his long life the previous year, had accorded its favourable award or not, it is certain that so early as the month of September, 1798, Thomas Campbell, in the *New Monthly Magazine*, gave a very favourable review of the plays, attributing them, however, to a man. This review won for them the attention and the admiration of many equally competent judges. A friendship was soon afterwards formed between Campbell and Joanna Baillie, which lasted without interruption to the close of their lives. She formed several similar friendships in the course of her life.

In the year 1799, a few days after she had written of the plays what has been quoted, Mary Berry announced that one of the tragedies was about to be acted. She refers to a rumour that the unknown author, on being applied to through Cadell, still "refuses to come forward even to receive emolument, and says the piece is before the public, and that the theatre may do what they please with it, only desiring that the simplicity of the plot may not be infringed upon. Neither fame nor a thousand pounds, therefore, have much effect on this said author's mind, whoever he or she may be. I say *she*, because, and only because, no man could or *would* draw such noble and dignified representations of the female mind as Countess Albini and Jane de Montfort. They often make us clever, captivating, heroic, but never *rationally* superior."

The author's refusing to come forward even to receive emolument, and her saying candidly that the piece was already before the public, reads very like an act of the Baillies in general, and of Joanna in particular; but her authorised biographer has taken no note of the circumstance. It might have been her first impulse, put aside on further reflection. On the other hand, the writer of the brief summary of Joanna's life alludes to her invariable practice with regard to her literary profits. Unlike Zaccheus the publican in every other respect, she followed his rule with respect to the earnings of her pen—half of her goods she gave to feed the poor. This arrangement was made and adhered to, when the Baillies' income, never a very large one, was at its minimum; and it was not departed from when increased funds brought in their train increased expenditure and a host of additional wants. During the family's stay at Long Calderwood, Mrs. Baillie could not forget that she was a minister's widow, and that this gave her poorer neighbours a claim on her feeling heart, planning head, and helping hand. Swallowed up in the "no man's" crowd of London, the women of the family must have found themselves mazed and baffled in their charitable commission, which they held both by their own choice and by inheritance. But still they were not women to neglect it, and Matthew Baillie's profession provided an opening for them. Later in life, when they were restored to something like the manageableness of a country district, deeds of charity became one great occupation of their united lives. Joanna describes Agnes as the almoner of the sisters :—

> "Take thy way,
> To gain, with hasty steps, some cottage door,
> On helpful errand to the neighbouring poor."

By some peculiarities of expression in the plays it oozed out that the author was Scotch; and a few hasty guessers hazarded the name of Mr. Scott, author of *Glenfinlas* and *The Eve of St. John*, in connection with the dramas which were so largely engaging the literary world. The more penetrating critics decided that the author was a woman, and the tide of public opinion had already set in for Mrs. John Hunter, when the dedication of the second volume to Dr. Matthew Baillie pointed to him

and his family as having a peculiar interest in
the author. The substitution of Mrs. Hunter
for Joanna Baillie, like a gold bodkin for a steel
dagger, sounds ludicrous to us; but the world
did not know aunt and niece in their respective
position to each other then. Lucy Aikin mentions
that while the question was still pending,
she met Joanna and Agnes Baillie making a
morning call. (It is queer, after all, to hear
of Joanna Baillie making a morning call in
a pelisse, beaver-hat, and feather.) The call
was at the house of Mrs. Barbauld, an excellent
woman, who was raised to as unchallenged
an eminence in the lettered circles of her own
day, as she is in danger of being undervalued
in another generation. The plays *par excellence*
were, of course, brought into discussion by so
fit a company, and the sister author of the
"Evenings at Home" praised them with all her
heart. But Joanna was not seduced into self-
betrayal even by "the sudden delight" which
Lucy Aikin believed such praise must have
afforded her. Lucy goes on to tell, that
"the faithful sister rushed forward, as we

afterwards recollected, to bear the brunt, while the unsuspected author lay snug in her taciturnity." But Joanna stood still more severe ordeals without losing her presence of mind, and that composure which was no more than decorum in her eyes.

Even when the curiosity of the refined Mrs. Grundy was satisfied with regard to the plays, which she had praised "hugely," she was reluctant to give all the credit to a middle-aged, middle-class, matter-of-fact woman, who had mixed little in society, and who knew practically nothing of the battle of life. Mrs. Grundy would still have it that "the introductory discourse," at least, was written by Joanna's exulting brother.

It was not till April, 1800, that the Scotch minister's daughter dared to come before the footlights, and ask an almost national—in some respects a more than national verdict, by having her play of *De Montfort* put on the great London stage of Drury Lane. Everything was done beforehand to ensure success. The scenery and decorations were to be appropriate and in the best style; the principal characters were to be splendidly represented by John Kemble and Sarah Siddons.

The brother and the sister Kemble, indeed, had taken a fancy to the brother and the sister characters in the play, which are said to have been cast expressly for the Kembles, the author having had the two in her mind. Before the Baillies removed to London, Mrs. Siddons had entered on her triumphs, and had become so much the rage, that, as one of the Misses Elliot of Minto—the witty and winning nieces of Miss Jean Elliot—wrote to her brother Hugh at Copenhagen, people of rank went and dined at the piazzas in Covent Garden at three o'clock, in order to get places, and "all the gentlemen cry, and the ladies are in fits." Thomas Campbell declared that Joanna Baillie had left "a perfect picture" of Mrs. Siddons in the description of Jane de Montfort :—

> *Page.* Madam, there is a lady in your hall,
> Who begs to be admitted to your presence.
> *Lady.* Is it not one of our invited friends?
> *Page.* No, far unlike to them; it is a stranger.
> *Lady.* How looks her countenance?

> *Page.* So, queenly, so commanding, and so noble,
> I shrank at first in awe ; but when she smiled,
> For so she did to see me thus abash'd,
> Methought I could have compass'd sea and land
> To do her bidding.
> *Lady.*   Is she young or old ?
> *Page.* Neither, if right I guess ; but she is fair ;
> For Time hath laid his hand so gently on her
> As he too had been awed.
> *Lady.*   The foolish stripling!
> She has bewitch'd thee. Is she large in stature ?
> *Page.* So stately and so graceful is her form,
> I thought at first her stature was gigantic ;
> But on a near approach I found, in truth,
> She scarcely does surpass the middle size.
> *Lady.* What is her garb ?
> *Page.* I cannot well describe the fashion of it.
> She is not deck'd in any gallant trim,
> But seems to me clad in the usual weeds
> Of high habitual state ; for as she moves,
> Wide flows her robe in many a waving fold,
> As I have seen unfurled banners play
> With a soft breeze.
> *Lady.*   Thine eyes deceive thee, boy ;
> It is an apparition thou hast seen.
> *Fuberg.* It is an apparition he has seen,
> Or it is Jane de Montfort.

One of the treats of the quiet household in Windmill Street must have been an occasional play.

The approbation of John Kemble and his sister was no slight flattery and no small promise of success. To add, if possible, to the actors' interest in the drama, a personal introduction was arranged. It seems that she who wove and they who wore the buskin in this instance took to each other heartily and stood by each other loyally. Either Mrs. Siddons had put off "the Catherine manner," as Mary Berry expressed her estimation of the great actress's high and uncertain humour in private company, or the "Catherine" tone had not jarred on Joanna as it did on the favourite of royal courts and salons. Joanna was herself a little formal in manner at first, in the same proportion that she was wonderfully simple and unexacting in character. Mrs. Siddons's speech to Joanna Baillie at the close of their first meeting, "Make me more Jane de Montforts," was still more gracious than her final condescension to Mary Berry and her friends, in singing to them in private and after supper.

Joanna, late in life, gave a more direct

expression of her deep admiration of Mrs. Siddons:—

> " The impassioned changes of thy beauteous face,
> Thy stately form and high, imperial grace;
> Thine arms impetuous toss'd, thy robe's wide flow,
> And the dark tempest gathered on thy brow,
> What time thy flashing eye and lip of scorn
> Down to the dust thy mimic foes have borne;
> Remorseful musings sunk to deep dejection,
> The fix'd and yearning looks of strong affection;
> The active turmoil a wrought bosom rending,
> Where pity, love, and honour are contending;—
> They, who beheld all this, right well I ween,
> A lovely, grand, and wondrous sight have seen.
>
> * * *
>
> Thy graceful form still moves in nightly dreams,
> And what thou wast to the lull'd sleeper seems;
> While feverish fancy oft doth fondly trace,
> Within her curtain'd couch thy wondrous face.
> Yea; and to many a wight, bereft and lone,
> In musing hours, though all to thee unknown,
> Soothing his earthly course of good and ill,
> With all thy potent charm thou actest still."

The prologue to *De Montfort* was written by the Hon. F. North, and the epilogue by the Duchess of Devonshire; so that rank and fashion might have some crumb to boast of in the fare.

But there is none to tell us how Joanna felt and looked at this great crisis of her fame. Was the impenetrable mask of her calmness at last rudely disturbed? Had she the courage to be present in a private box, to sit out either the acclamations which should crown her with renown, or the derision which should cover her with something like disgrace? Or did she depute her almost equally interested brother to be present, to see and hear for her? Did she wait the fiat in his house, or did she sit at her own quiet fireside, not caring so very much to hide her trembling there, unless it were that her firmness might compose the agitation of Mrs. Baillie and Agnes? Could Joanna not quite shut out, by absence and closed eyelids, the sea of upturned faces in the pit? Did her precise woman's nose smart at the smell of the sawdust and the orange peel? Did she think of her countryman, James Thomson, and how the scales of fortune were reversed in his case by one unlucky line—

"O! Sophonisba, Sophonisba, O!"—

caught up by the terrible wags in the galleries, and parodied with the shout:—

"O! Jemmy Thomson, Jemmy Thomson, O!"

Did she remember Oliver Goldsmith and his open tremors and quavers? Though we are sure that Joanna's mood bore no resemblance to that of the outrageous little Irishman, we should like to know what she thought at the moment the curtain was drawing up that night on "the large, old-fashioned chamber in Jordan's house," with "Jerome entering, bearing a light, followed by Manuel and servants carrying luggage."

Without question, Joanna's faith in her great and good aim of reforming the drama, as well as of exercising her gift, must have supported her. Without doubt, she was not unduly oppressed, any more than unduly elated; but she was a woman, after all, and her spirit must have been up in arms that night.

De Montfort was well received by a large and appreciative audience. But its radical defects as a stage-play prevented it, even in the powerful hands of the Kembles, from holding its place for more than eleven nights. Thomas Campbell might well say that it abounded in beautiful passages; but all its noble feeling and fine eloquence could not compensate for its author's ignorance of stage effect. The principle which she had acted on, of making the interest to centre in the hearts and not in the circumstances of the *dramatis personæ*, was disastrous so far as the theatre was concerned. The rapid withdrawal of the piece was a disappointment to all concerned. But there were compensations to its author. Her work had met with general regard, and the more distinguished the critics, for the most part, the more weighty their approbation. *De Montfort* had not been written with a direct view to the stage. And if the stage were all wrong and wanted reformation, that desirable end was not to be accomplished by one play, or the bringing out of that play.

By the autumn of 1801, from the date of a note which has been preserved, Joanna and her mother and sister must have established themselves at Hampstead. For six or seven years

they were on Red Lion Hill. One does not
need to say that Hampstead with its breezy
heath was much more of a rural suburb then
than it is now. The district between it and
London offered a tempting opportunity for high-
waymen. Sir Walter Scott recounted, as a
sharp test of his courage, on one occasion, the
sudden starting up before him of a very sus-
picious figure, just when he had become conscious of the misfortune of having lost his way,
and of being benighted in the labyrinth of lanes
and fields about Hampstead.

To the country-bred women who had been
for sixteen years pent up among stone and lime,
the settling at Hampstead was like a return to
all natural wholesome pleasure. Yet to natives
of Clyde's and Calder's banks, who had looked
up at Tinto and shivered before "the long
whang" of Carnwath Muir, Highgate and the
Heath could not but have been decidedly tame.
The traditions of Harrow, which Byron had left
only recently, and of Finchley with its Dick Tur-
pin heroes in crape masks and boots and tights
—unless, indeed, one went as far as Barnet and

the Middle Ages—shrank and paled before the legends of Drumclog Covenanters, and of brownies and bogles and fairies dancing on the Fairy Knowe. But Hampstead had one unapproachable advantage to a thoughtful spirit like Joanna's. She could receive inspiration from looking down on the outlines of the mass of buildings which betokened the presence of the great congregation of London, and from listening to its muffled myriad voices sounding faintly in the air. Joanna's eyes turned always and at all seasons towards London. Her gaze did not fix on the grass, the gorse, and the trees among which she often sauntered and sat, alone or in congenial companionship, for hours at a stretch; but turned continually towards the great city. She herself tells in her verse how her attention wandered away to—

> "Towers, belfries, lengthened streets, and structures fair.
> St. Paul's high dome amidst the vassal bands
> Of neighbouring spires, a regal chieftain stands;
> And over fields of ridgy roofs appear,
> With distance softly tinted, side by side,
> In kindred grace, like twain of sisters dear,
> The towers of Westminster, her abbey's pride.
> * * * *

> Viewed thus, a goodly sight! but when surveyed
> Through denser air, when moistened winds prevail,
> In her grand panoply of smoke arrayed,
> While clouds aloft in heavy volumes sail,
> She is sublime—she seems a curtain'd doom
> Connecting heaven and earth,—a threatening sign of doom.
>
>   *   *   *   *
>
>   Through drizzly rain,
> Cataracts of tawny sheen pour from the skies,
> Of furnace smoke black curling volumes rise!
> And many-tinted vapours slowly pass
> O'er the wide draping of that pictured mass.
>
> So shows by day this grand imperial town;
> And, when o'er all the night's black stole is thrown,
> The distant traveller doth with wonder mark
> Her luminous canopy athwart the dark,
> Cast up from myriads of lamps, that shine
> Along her streets in many a starry line,
> He wondering looks from his yet distant road,
> And thinks the Northern streamers are abroad.
> ' What hollow sound is that?' Approaching near,
> The roar of many wheels breaks on his ear;
> It is the flood of human life in motion!
> It is the voice of a tempestuous ocean.
> With sad but pleasing awe his soul is fill'd,—
> Scarce heaves his breast, and all within is still'd,
> As many thoughts and feelings cross his mind—
> Thoughts mingled, melancholy, undefined,
> Of restless, reckless man, and years gone by,
> And Time fast wending to Eternity."

At Hampstead the Baillies found themselves

amongst a set of neighbours remarkable, like the Clapham circle, for their worth and benevolence. These neighbours and the Baillies took to each other very kindly. In addition, at Hampstead the Baillies were able to practise something of their old country hospitality to chance or wayfaring guests. Matthew would look in and get a bed for a night, on his way to a country patient, while Matthew's wife and little ones would come out for longer benefit from country quarters.

Joanna, the famous author, was also the energetic purveyor and arranger of family and neighbourly feasts. Stars from the great world were constantly appearing at the Baillies' table, attracted by the fame and the wit of Joanna—it may have been fascinated too by the graceful and curious information of Agnes Baillie, who was a remarkable and very attractive woman, a fit pendant to her sister.

Hampstead saw the beginning and the crowning completion of many peculiarly happy and sympathetic friendships in Joanna Baillie's history. Lucy Aikin came with her mother. After leaving it for a time, when she was advanced in life she returned with a longing to die and be buried in the locality. Mr. Richardson (Sir Walter's "Johnnie Richardson") journeyed from Edinburgh, and pitched his tent at Hampstead. He soon formed one of the attractions that drew Sir Walter, the kindliest and homeliest of great men, from the din and whirl of London to enjoy with his old friend and his new friend—the ex-lawyer and the poetess—their peaceful, Scotch-kept Sundays at Hampstead. Miss Noel (Milbanke), in the serene spring of her girlhood, and throughout the stormy summer of Lady Byron's matronhood, was Joanna Baillie's dear and highly-valued friend.

Before November, 1801, Joanna had made the acquaintance of Mary Berry, and had advanced so far towards intimacy with her, that she wrote the prologue and the epilogue for Mary's amateur play of *Fashionable Friends*. There can hardly be a doubt that Miss Baillie witnessed the private theatricals played by aristocratic performers at Strawberry Hill. It must have seemed to her very like playing at work. And that fairy palace—half gem, half toy, so much more costly in many respects than another fairy palace which she was yet to inhabit with greater sympathy—wanted its high presiding genius before Joanna crossed its threshold. Probably it did not much matter, so far as she was concerned. To the exquisite critic, Horace Walpole, notwithstanding that he affected her graceful Aunt Hunter, Joanna at this date was likely to be as distasteful as Dr. Johnson had proved repulsive to the Horace Walpole of old.

One cannot help thinking that, with all Mary Berry's patronage and petting, Joanna was a little out of place in connection with such a game of a play. Certainly if she had not recognised the fact, she might have appeared once and again in such society; and, had she chosen to forsake old friends and to adapt herself to new associates, she would have been moulded and fused into the society, as one of the privileged *habituées* of its inner intellectual circle.

In 1802 Joanna Baillie published her second volume of "Plays of the Passions." It contained a comedy on hatred; *Ethwald*, a tragedy on ambition, in two parts; and a comedy on ambition. With mingled consistency and inconsistency, she followed the example of the Stuarts, and would not be taught by experience. In spite of her penetration and her power of painting human nature, she adhered rigidly to her plan of writing both a tragedy and a comedy on the growth of a single passion—with its working in the heart, spreading outwardly, and controlling circumstances, not being controlled by them. She continued to insist that the analysis of a passion in itself and in its results, ought to be the true source of the spectator's terror, pity, or mirth.

In July of the same year Mr. Jeffrey made his well-known attack on the plays in the *Edinburgh Review*. He handled them freely, and exposed their weak points with a criticism not only searching, but galling. He maintained that Joanna Baillie's theory, so far as it was original, was arbitrary and false, because of the complex nature of man's moral constitution, and the powerful influence exerted upon it by fellow creatures and by contemporary events. He argued that there was no ground for a higher aim in the drama than the entertainment of the audience. For that end fortunes and misfortunes were as effectual as feelings and principles. He scouted the idea of men being induced to crush passion in the germ within their own breasts by watching its rise in the breasts of others. He pointed to the excesses of passion as being frequently the abuse of virtues which, in their germ, should be fostered in place of being crushed. Even if a play on a single passion were legitimate art, he alleged that the limits of one play were too narrow to show its development in a natural and convincing manner. At the same time he admitted Joanna Baillie's grasp of character and her painstaking work; but he accused her of making a raw-head and bloody-bones employment of slaughter, while she professed to despise scenic incident. He charged her, not simply with imitation of Shakspeare, but with direct plagiarism from him, and with slavish borrowing and reproducing of his obsolete words and turns of speech.

Few people will endorse the whole of Jeffrey's criticism now. In after days he himself greatly qualified it. Its general justness as well as poignancy is, however, as plain now as then. The great ability of the reviewer, together with the tyrannous supremacy of censorship to which the *Edinburgh Review* had attained, made the hostile verdict formidable. Although Joanna allowed little sign to manifest itself, the criticism cut to the quick of her susceptibility to praise and blame. But Jeffrey's criticism could not conquer her any more than her gallant and obstinate resistance could disarm him.

During the year 1804 Joanna published her volume of "Miscellaneous Plays." Perhaps unconsciously she had been influenced by Jeffrey's critique to the extent of modifying her theory and of allowing the plays a freer construction; but she denied the fact stoutly in her preface. The concession, if such it could be called, was of small moment in softening Jeffrey's hostility.

In the *Edinburgh Review* for January, 1805, he had another article on "Miss Baillie's 'Miscellaneous Plays.'" In this article he frankly admitted that "Miss Baillie cannot possibly write a tragedy, nor an act of a tragedy, without showing genius and exemplifying a more dramatic conception and expression than any of her modern competitors." He could not help quoting largely, with extorted commendation, from her beautiful and moving play of *Constantine Palæologus*, which was taking the rest of the world by storm. At the same time Jeffrey's strictures on the defects of the plays were, if possible, more severe than in the previous encounter, and his tone had acquired something of supercilious arrogance and positive animus.

But Joanna was not without a compensation. From the same year, 1804, she dated her meeting with another Scotchman, more purely a man of letters, who viewed her and her plays in a different spirit from that in which Jeffrey regarded them. Sir Walter Scott was up in London, and having a great sympathy with his countrywoman, and a sincere admiration of her work, he got an introduction to her through their common friend Mr. Sotheby, the translator of "Oberon," whose acquaintance Sir Walter had made many years before, when Mr. Sotheby was an officer in a regiment stationed at Edinburgh. Joanna was fresh from Mr. Scott's "Lay of the Last Minstrel," and very likely he was fresh from her *Constantine.*

Joanna may have felt a momentary disappointment in seeing a plain, somewhat heavy lawyer's face as the face of her poet; and it might also flash across his mind, that the kind, sensible, very original, but very lean little Scotchwoman who received him was not his ideal of the tragic muse. But their intercourse was thenceforth honourable alike to their heads and hearts, and was brotherly and sisterly.

In 1806, when Joanna was forty-four years of age, she and Agnes had the grief of parting from their mother. Mrs. Baillie had attained a ripe age, and had been for some time declining in health. She had been stone-blind for years, and was latterly paralytic. The sisters watched her by day and by night. Joanna, who was the great nurse of the household, and had the distinct qualification that she did not suffer from loss of sleep, took the heaviest share of nursing. There was much to soften the blow, but to the clinging household of women it was a blow still. When, more than ten years after, Joanna wrote to Mary Berry the letter in which she condoles with her on the death of her father, there is a lingering remembrance of that parting.

With their mission for the time gone, and the ache of a void at their hearth, the sisters resolved to revisit Scotland, which they had quitted twenty-one years before. They spent some months there in the years 1807—8. They went directly to their native place, to rest among their old friends of the fruit lands and of Glasgow. They scrambled on Clyde's banks, and paced the Trongate once more. To the friends whom they had left behind them, these middle-aged women came back with all the prestige which Joanna had won for them. If she had been found capable of inspiring awe when she was but a girl of fifteen in her father's old college days, it could hardly be doubted that she would now be an alarming Joanna Baillie to the foolish and frivolous of all ages. It was so to a certain extent, though it was a case of consciences taking guilt to themselves. It is Lucy Aikin's volunteered testimony that Joanna was only too tolerant of impertinence. Old friends were inclined for a moment to protest that the lively, warm-hearted girl on whom years and fame had fallen, reappeared a proud, cold woman. But the protest was only entered when the friends could not make sufficient allowance for certain difficulties of Joanna's position,—for the effects of time and trial, and for the elements of sadness in a first return to the scenes of youth after a long absence. The same friends soon remarked with astonishment that the London Miss Baillies—Joanna quite as much as Agnes—came back speaking broader Scotch and making use of more Scotch phrases than when they went away. Without fail, these jealous friends were not long of comprehending and congratulating themselves on the discovery that, when she was alone with them, Joanna was the very same unaffected and reliable friend she had ever been; and that she had a particular delight in reverting to old stories and old adventures.

Joanna's temporary residence in Glasgow was marked by a kind, womanly exercise of her leisure, taste, and influence. Hearing that a visit from her would be very welcome, she went and saw Struthers, the shoemaker poet. She looked over and expressed cordial admiration for his MS. poem of the "Poor Man's Sabbath." By her instrumentality and that of Sir Walter Scott, whom she enlisted in his cause, she induced Mr. Constable to publish the poem; and, though its success was very partial, and the money which it brought its author not above thirty or forty pounds, she did what she could to make public his talents and merits,—an act which was in the end profitable to Struthers. In this manner she certainly gladdened the heart of a gifted and worthy man.

Another publication of this year, in which Joanna had the greatest interest, was Sir Walter's "Marmion." She was imparting her delight in the perusal of the book by reading it aloud for the first time in a circle of friends, when she was startled by coming to the following passage:—

> .... "the wild harp that silent hung
> By silver Avon's holy shore
> 'Till twice an hundred years rolled o'er.
> When she the bold enchantress came,
> With fearless hand and heart in flame,
> From the pale willow snatched the treasure,
> And swept it with a kindred measure;
> Till Avon's swans, while rang the grove
> With Montfort's hate and Basil's love,
> Awakening at the inspirèd strain,
> Deemed their own Shakspeare lived again."

Thrilled to her heart's heart by this tribute of praise from a source which she prized above all others, the indomitable, great little woman read the passage to the end without pause or faltering, and only displayed a want of self-command when the emotion of a friend who was present (her attached sister Agnes?) became uncontrollable.

Joanna and her sister left Glasgow to make a tour in the West Highlands, which they had not visited before. Brought face to face with the sublime features of nature which she loved so well, she relaxed her guard on the expression of her feelings, and indulged in greater self-abandonment than she had ever allowed herself to indulge in before. She was so overcome as to shed tears as she gazed on the Falls of Moness. She would not be torn away from the sight and sound for an hour, though she was drenched by the rain, which fell heavily during the entire time that she was in the glen.

In the spring of 1808,—the season of the year when "mine own romantic town" is in the perfection of its picturesque buildings and gardens, and still more picturesque environs,— the sisters took their way to Edinburgh. The intellectual society of the Scotch metropolis was ready with a great demonstration to welcome an illustrious countrywoman who had brought much honour to Scotland. The Baillies found their home under the most choice roof in the city—the roof of Sir Walter—at 39, Castle Street, where they confirmed a close and affectionate intimacy with the master and every member of the family down even to the dogs. Lord Jeffrey, under the auspices of the Duchess of Gordon, sought to afford to the world the polite spectacle of exchange of courtesies with his foe. Joanna must have burnt with curiosity to know the brilliant reviewer whom Lucy Aikin thought the only amusing man in Edinburgh, who united French *esprit* to English industry, and who, when he got into a scrape with a hot-blooded Irishman, did not decline to fight a duel to clear it up. But, to her woman's sore heart, in conflict with her unflinching spirit, Jeffrey's flag of truce was but the egotism of a hardened offender. She resolutely and rudely —at all events bluntly—resisted his overtures and the entreaties of mediating friends. She absolutely refused an introduction to the king of critics, and defied his thunderbolts in future *Edinburgh Reviews*. She did not hesitate to declare her reason. Mr. Jeffrey's articles had given her much pain, and caused great disadvantage to her works. "*She considered them written with a desire to exalt the fame of the critic and the popularity of the periodical, without due regard to justice and propriety of feeling."* If Mr. Jeffrey so erred, he was by no means the last critic who deserved to be confronted with such an error. As for Joanna, however little she was accustomed to wear her heart on her sleeve, she could no more dissemble her feelings than the weakest woman. She swept past her antagonist with a simple majesty of innocent wrath, which left him smiling and shrugging his shoulders, but in his not ungenerous heart just a little touched.

In this visit to the North, Joanna Baillie and Mary Berry crossed each other. The latter expresses her wish that there had been some "setting and footing together in the course of the jigging about." In August Mary Berry was with Lady Douglas at Bothwell Castle, and recounted her pilgrimage to Joanna's birthplace. "What a pretty place Millheugh is! I walked all down the rocky bed of the river below the bridge, and crossed over the 'stepping-stones' and back again, merely for the pleasure of doing it, and then went all round the house at Millheugh, and to the wooden bridge which looks at the little cascade up the green walk by the side of the stream. We saw not a human creature, either to welcome or forbid us their premises, which being all open we committed no trespass. I tried the echoes with some lines of *Basil;* but they were dumb, only muttered in return for your name, something about muslin at Glasgow, a pattern of a handkerchief, and some stories of the poor in the villages. Your heroic muse should have taught them better in such a romantic spot.

"I have been over, too, at my own dear little ravine at Blantyre; and if you go there again, you will see Berina (my name in Arcadia) cut upon one of the largest trees by my own fair hand on the 20th August, 1808."

Early next spring, that of 1809, the great Drury Lane Theatre, where "the other year" Joanna had staked so many hopes and fears, was burned to the ground.

A little later she had it in her power to return some of Sir Walter's hospitalities. He was in London then, starting the *Quarterly Review*, and had brought up Mrs. Scott, and their little daughter Sophia. Mr. and Mrs. Scott stayed with their good old French friends, the Dumergues, the surgeon-dentist's family in Piccadilly; but the ten-years-old little girl was sent out, in order to save her rosy cheeks, to Hampstead, to the kind care of the Misses Baillie. Little Sophia, as she helped Miss Agnes in her garden, or trotted by Miss Joanna's side on the Heath, must have renewed remote and recent associations by her chatter of the knowes and the haughs and the deep Tweed pools; of hunting and fishing with papa and Charlie, and running with little Annie and the dogs, in her happy holidays at Ashiestiel. The divided family party were often reunited. There must have been many a cheerful supper and breakfast out at Hampstead, many a merry rendezvous and lunch with Dr. Matthew Baillie's family, then in Cavendish Square. Dainty, dogmatic Mary Berry was not too dignified to be eager to renew her acquaintance with Mr. Scott. She had already met and held "long conversations" with him at Bothwell Castle and at Minto. On the 1st of June he was at a breakfast party at the Berrys, in North Audley Street, meeting among other company, Sir George Beaumont and Lady Louisa Stewart. Somebody was to read Joanna Baillie's tragedy of *The Family Legend*, which had a particular interest for Miss Berry, having been founded on an incident in the family history of her friend Mrs. Damer, which had been related by Mrs. Damer to Joanna. As nobody but Mary Berry was sufficiently acquainted with Joanna's handwriting, Mary was the somebody who read the tragedy on the occasion of the breakfast in North Audley Street. Mary Berry and Joanna Baillie interchanged such " courtesies " as the reading of each other's MSS., in which courtesies Miss Berry showed an inclination to be her own reader. According to Mary Berry's journal for this April, Joanna came on another morning to North Audley Street, when Mary read to her friend her notice of Madame Dudevant's life. Mary wrote afterwards in her journal that Joanna was so pleased with the notice of the life, that she could not but feel very much flattered. Miss Berry then went, probably in Joanna Baillie's company, "to

Walter Scott's, where I saw his wife for the first time." This was at the Dumergues', who might also have had something to say worth hearing as to French lives and letters; but Mary Berry fails to chronicle the remarks of the surgeon-dentist's family.

Sir Walter's letters to Joanna Baillie are from this time frequent, full, and instinct with the man's brotherly heart. He laboured with a will in her service, and accomplished for her the acceptance by Henry Siddons, for the Edinburgh Theatre, of her play, *The Family Legend;* and next, he secured the putting of it upon the stage with more undeniable success than attended the representation of *De Montfort* at Drury Lane.

Five years before, while Joanna was much occupied with her infirm mother, Mrs. Damer told Joanna the story of *The Family Legend*. Joanna wanted a subject for a drama, and wanted, also, some diversion at spare moments. She dramatised the story. Very likely her tour two years afterwards in the West Highlands—although she might not go so far as Mull—was undertaken with some idea of authenticating the scenery of the legend. It was then remarked that Joanna lost no opportunity of entering Highland huts, and of rendering herself familiar with Highland manners and customs. In the end she had a peculiar fondness for this drama, calling it her Highland play, and exulting in its success.

Sir Walter spared no effort that devotion to the author's interest could suggest. He was in constant consultation with Mr. Siddons on the costumes and machinery of the play. He attended every rehearsal, changed names (to obviate the apprehended spleen of the clan Maclean), smoothed difficulties, wooed and coaxed magnates, and wrote the prologue, while Henry Mackenzie wrote the epilogue. He was prominently responsible in his place all through the trying first night, while Mrs. Scott, recalling her early passion for theatricals, did her duty by heading a box thirty friends strong. Finally he was happy to be able to proclaim to the person most interested, the enthusiastic reception of the piece, and its announcement

for the rest of the week. No wonder that
Joanna Baillie loved Sir Walter, and Sir
Walter loved Joanna. Such an abandonment of kindness is, as Joanna once quoted,
"the cords of a man" to knit friend to
friend. In effect, *The Family Legend* was not
acted more than fourteen nights in Edinburgh;
but it was received there with a favour which
none of Joanna Baillie's plays received in
London. And it is a suggestive fact, that in
Edinburgh, where she had no powerful ally save
Scott, but where the audience was select and
highly cultivated, Joanna Baillie's work was
more fully appreciated than on any London
stage.

Later the same year, Sir Walter's holidays
were spent among the Hebrides in company with
his wife, his elder girl, his dog Wallace, and a
few friends. From Ulva House he wrote to his
"cummer" Joanna, because he could not resist
writing to her in places which she had rendered
classic and immortal. He gave her a spirited
account of the Ladies' Rock, the scene of the
exposure of Helen in the legend of Dunstaffnage

and Staffa. He made a blithe summary of the landing in which Charlotte lost her shoes, and little Sophia her collection of pebbles; and of the boating, in which "all the ladies were sick, especially Hannah Mackenzie," adding triumphantly, "and none of the gentlemen escaped except Staffa and myself." He begged to tell her that he had picked up for her a hallowed green pebble from the shore of St. Columba, — but the piper was sounding to breakfast.

In the meantime Joanna had the pleasure of visiting her brother at the estate which he had bought in Gloucestershire. Well won and well worn were Matthew Baillie's medical honours and gains. He had his uncle's post as a Court physician, and was at this time watching—fruitlessly, in both cases—the lingering decline of Princess Amelia, and the final relapse into madness of "the poor king." Much need had Dr. Baillie of his Gloucestershire retreat, though he could pay but flying visits to it. Joanna made one "very dear friend" in that neighbourhood, Justina Milligan, of Cotswold House, whose death she commemorates in one of the last of her writings. Justina was a kindly, cheerful woman, dwelling in a sisterly household like Joanna's own, dispensing her larger gifts of fortune, as Joanna and Agnes dispensed their modest income, with much feeling regard to the poor. And Justina shared Agnes Baillie's love of gardening—the true love which does not confine itself to the service of hired hands, nor call every spot of earth common and unclean save the trim garden and the costly greenhouse. Joanna celebrates a pet spot of Justina's:—

> "Nor did such toward spots alone declare
> Her pleasing fancy and her skilful care;
> The long-neglected quarry, grim and gray,
> Where rubbish in uncouth confusion lay,
> Loose stones and sand, with weeds and brush-wood rotten,
> And everything or worthless or forgotten,
> Seemed to obey her will, as though by duty
> Constrained, and soon became a place of beauty.
> Its fairy floor is mossy green,
> And o'er its creviced walls, I ween,
> The harebell, foxglove, fern and heather,
> Mingle most lovingly together;
> While from the upper screen, as bent to see
> What might be hid below, the rowan tree
> And drooping birch seem to look curiously;

> A friendly place, where birds for shelter come,
> And bees, and flies, and moths raise a soft summer hum.
> Justina's quarry! a name most dear,
> Will henceforth sweetly, sadly soothe the ear."*

Either before or after Joanna's visit to Gloucestershire, Elizabeth Hamilton revisited London, and spent some days at Hampstead. There the friendship between her and Joanna Baillie was renewed. Their letters afterwards gradually drop the "Madam," or the friends reproach each other with the use of it. They become more and more cordial and confidential. We have only specimens of the correspondence on Mrs. Hamilton's side; but it is a pleasant glimpse which we get of an old friendship in old letters. In one letter Mrs. Hamilton describes the Hunterian Museum in Glasgow, and recurs to a lady whom she remembers as a schoolgirl at Miss Macdonald's. In another, she speaks of fancying herself in the little drawing-room at Hampstead, with one sister on the couch by her side, the other in the snug corner opposite to her, while she herself is

---
* Written after Justina Milligan's death.

deliberately putting her feet on the fender for a social " crack." In a third letter, the author of the "Cottagers of Glenburnie" vows that the next time the author of the "Plays of the Passions" visits Scotland, she will insist on taking her to Aberdeen; quoting an anecdote of an old gentleman who had travelled twice through Europe, and had never seen anything to be compared to Aberdeen but—the bay of Naples. Mrs. Hamilton prophesies that if Walter Scott would open the cry about Aberdeen, as he had done about Loch Katrine scenery, how the world would be deafened by reiterated praises!

Among many weightier reflections, Elizabeth Hamilton congratulates Joanna on the happy effect of Joanna's patches on the sofa-cover. Mrs. Hamilton even playfully suggests that a notary ought to have registered the performance in a national record, and demands, "What would a stocking" (she might have said a sock more appropriately), "darned by the hands of Shakspeare, now bring to the lucky owner?"

By November Sir Walter had his Iona pebble or pebbles cut and set as a brooch, in the form of a Scotch harp, with the inscription in Gaelic, "Buail o'n tend" ("Strike the string"), and he sent the brooch as a keepsake to Joanna, with a "God give you joy to wear it." Much did Joanna prize the characteristic gift, and in the earliest and best portrait we have of her, Sir Walter's brooch is represented as fastening her collar.

In May, 1811, Mary Berry went down to Hampstead to stay from Saturday till Monday, and tried the novelty of dining before four o'clock in her friend's simple little household, and of going out on the Heath after dinner and sitting there for above two hours in a "delicious fine evening." Afterwards she and Joanna read over together one of Mary Berry's longer pieces, and criticised it. Some of her other scraps (that she seems to have carried with her for the purpose) were also read and criticised, Mary Berry stating, with her customary frankness, "which I think Joanna liked less than I expected." On

Sunday the friends sat by the fire the whole day, and Joanna gave the others her drama on Hope to read. It was in two acts only, and Mary soon read it. "Very poetical," she commented in her turn (journalising), "and much fancy, as all her things have; but this did not equal my expectation—how high it was I know not. It is certainly a sufficiently dramatic story, but not dramatically managed."

The letters between Edinburgh and Ashiestiel on the one hand, and Hampstead on the other, during the following year, are full of details with regard to Sir Walter's having become a laird on Tweed-side. His earlier, gleeful projects for Abbotsford, beginning so modestly with the cottage having "two spare bed-rooms with dressing-rooms, each of which will, on a pinch, have a couch bed," are also significantly dwelt upon.

Joanna writes: "If I should ever be happy enough to be at Abbotsford, you must take me to see Ashiestiel too. I have a kind of tenderness for it, as one has for a man's first wife, when you hear he has married a second."

In 1811, ere the volume was before the public and subjected to the critics, Joanna sent to Sir Walter an early copy of her third volume of the "Plays of the Passions." It contains *Orra* and *The Dream*, two tragedies, and *The Siege*, a comedy on Fear, with *The Beacon*, a musical drama on Hope. She declared that it was to be her last publication, and that she was getting her knitting needles in order—meaning to begin her new course of industry with a purse for her friend, in return for his Iona brooch. Sir Walter was enchanted with the last plays. He read *Orra* twice to himself, and had Terry, the actor, to read it to him, in a sympathetic circle, a third time. In January, 1812, Sir Walter sent Joanna an ancient silver mouth-piece, to which she might adapt his purse. He protested that this was a genteel way of tying her down to her promise; and he engaged, on his part, that the purse should not hold bank notes or vulgar bullion, but pretty little medals and nicknackets. He ended a long letter by a very frank reference to his bargains with his publishers and the state of his affairs. In April, when one of the hardest

Border springs on record was signalising itself by mail coaches stopped and shepherds lost in the snow, the arrival of "the elegant and acceptable token of your regard" was duly acknowledged by Sir Walter, and a full and serious letter on the comparative advantages of London and Edinburgh society, on her literary prospects and on his, and on Lord Byron's "Childe Harold," was closed with a list of the contents of the purse as they then stood:—

"1st. Miss Elizabeth Baillie's" (Matthew's daughter) "purse penny" (sent to prevent the purse's travelling empty), "called by the learned a denarius of the Empress Faustina.

"2nd. A gold brooch found in a bog in Ireland, which, for aught I know, fastened the mantle of an Irish princess in the days of Cuthullen or Neal of the Nine Hostages.

"3rd. A toadstone—a celebrated amulet, which was never lent to any one, unless upon a bond for a thousand marks for its being safely restored. It was sovereign for protecting new-born children and their mothers from the power of the fairies, and has been repeatedly borrowed from my mother on account of this virtue.

"4th. A coin of Edward I., found in Dryburgh Abbey.

"5th. A funeral ring, with Dean Swift's hair.

"So, you see," Sir Walter winds up the catalogue gallantly, "my nicknackatory is well supplied, though the purse is more valuable than all its contents."

In that triumphant war year of 1812, when illuminated London, seen from Hampstead, must have stood out often against the sky like a crown of carbuncles, Joanna wished to learn the mind of the *Edinburgh Review*, whether it remained the same towards her, or whether it had changed. She had not to wait long, and the oracle gave no doubtful sound. Sir Walter, to soften the blow—if it could be called so, after what had gone before—had written that he had been told Jeffrey talked very favourably of this latest volume however. Sir Walter added, "I should be glad, for his own sake, that he took some opportunity to retrace the paths of his criticism; but after pledging himself so deeply as he has done, I doubt much his giving way even unto conviction." Sir Walter's doubts were fulfilled. In the *Edinburgh Review* for February Mr. Jeffrey out-Heroded Herod, in his effort to crush Joanna Baillie's theory and practice. He prefaced his article by reminding Miss Baillie and the public, with an almost pompous and an entirely autocratic solemnity, that, in spite of his previous admonitions, she had gone on (as he had expected) in her own way, and had become (as he had expected) both less popular and less deserving of popularity in every successive publication. He then entered into a masterly analysis of ancient Greek and modern French dramatic literature, comparing these with the masterpieces of the English stage, and making out to his own satisfaction that Joanna Baillie had managed to combine the faults of all schools. Not content with accusing her of tameness, slowness, and awkwardness in the business of the plays—comparing it to travelling through a dull stage in the central Scottish Highlands—he deliberately denied to her the power of delineating individual character, on which as he alleged, she built, with undue confidence, her claims as a dramatist. He charged her at once with heaviness and poverty of style; he impugned her judgment, her taste, and her musical ear. After he had found so much to condemn, it becomes hard to guess what he could discover to praise; but he did suffer himself to accredit her with moral purity, considerable knowledge of human nature, and good sense. He almost excepted in his strictures the little drama on Hope, which had not taken Mary Berry's fancy, though its merits certainly did not consist in the fable, nor in the delineation of character. Finally he admitted that he had stumbled on fine passages, few and far between in the plays; and he recorded that "Miss Baillie's forte was in the delineation of horror"—though she did it coarsely. From such a verdict, at once cold-blooded and sweeping, there was no appeal. Joanna, like Wordsworth, resigned herself to bear the brunt of a perpetual feud with the *Edinburgh Review* and its formidable staff, thankful for one small mercy, that she had not consented to waive her honest feelings, and make the acquaintance of Mr. Jeffrey when she was in Edinburgh.

At a small party given by Miss Berry in North Audley Street, in June, 1813, Joanna made one of the ten ladies who, well supported by twenty-six gentlemen, were honoured with invitations to meet Madame de Staël. We do not have Joanna's version of the impression left on her by the swarthy, impassioned, ambitious Corinne. But we find Mary Berry scribbling that Joanna had been less reserved than usual, and was much pleased with Madame de Staël; and again that Madame de Staël did not know what to make of a person whose life was so totally different from her own. In truth, few literary women could have stood—alike in their antecedents and nurture—nearer to the antipodes from each other, than she who was born in the manse of Bothwell and matured in the doctor's house in Windmill Street, and she who grew up amid the philosophic discussions of the salons of Paris, the tempest of the great French Revolution, and whose career culminated in an attempt to raise a centre of political influence in opposition to that of Napoleon Bonaparte.

Further on in the year, another literary woman, with whom Joanna had more in common, and who became, indeed, her fast friend, came up to town. This was Maria Edgeworth, in company with her father and his fourth wife, her young stepmother.

Maria Edgeworth's winning warmth and vivacity, with its backbone of sound sense, broke down the barrier of Joanna Baillie's caution and shyness. The grave, silent Scotchwoman was fascinated, and her own dry native humour flowed and sparkled. It was "Maria" and "Joanna" between them in a very short time. Sir Walter, too, submitted willingly to the spell exercised by the keen, tiny Irishwoman. He declared that her quaint, fairy-like appearance, reminded him of the "whippit stourie" of nursery tales. It caught his sense of drollery; while her naïvete and ardour delighted him. The easy, unaffected manner in which she carried her well-deserved fame, secured his respect and admiration. She and Joanna Baillie were thenceforth correspondents not less intimate and regular than were Joanna and Sir Walter.

In 1813, Mrs. Elizabeth Hamilton writes to Joanna, describing a tour which she and her sister had made in Wales, and a visit they had paid to the two ladies then masquerading as hermits in a nook of the principality. In 1814, while Joanna's friend Sir Walter was voyaging to Orkney, Joanna and her sister followed Mrs. Hamilton's and Mrs. Blake's example, receiving the mock condolence of the former for losing, in the interest of blue mountains and foaming waterfalls, the crush fêtes with which London celebrated the presence of the allied princes, and at which these august men and their womankind occasionally "showed their backs."

In the same letter, Elizabeth Hamilton asks Joanna if she had heard of "Waverley," a novel supposed to be by the pen of Walter Scott. Mrs. Hamilton had only seen the first volume, but was so charmed with it that she was all impatience for the remainder. She takes it for granted that Joanna had, of course, seen the "Queen's Wake." In a letter from the same good judge next year, she exclaims in exultation, " Let no one say that imagination does not operate on this side of the Tweed! What do you think of 'Discipline?' of 'Waverley?' of 'Guy Mannering?' .... The two last are portrait pieces of first-rate excellence; the painter, a Gerard Dow,—not a Michael Angelo, —but in his own peculiar department coming near perfection. Though the name of Scott does not grace the title-page, it is seen in every other page of both performances."

This was nearly the last letter which Elizabeth Hamilton wrote to Joanna Baillie. In one other, Mrs. Hamilton touches on some troubles which were harassing her last days. She does not forget to record how much she had been pleased with the description a Professor Y. had given her of Joanna's niece, Matthew's daughter. The two friends had anticipated from this quarter a harvest of happiness, which one of them lived to reap; and Elizabeth Hamilton, whose own expectations in somewhat similar circumstances appear to have been thwarted and her hopes disappointed, still does not fail to congratulate Joanna on her brighter experience, and to moralise sagely on the satisfactory result that young Miss Baillie's gifts and graces were not spoiled "by the varnish of affectation and conceit."

Yes, Joanna knew "Waverley" and "Guy Mannering," though "Abbotsford and Kaeside," had not taken her formally into his confidence any more than he had taken the immediate members of his own family. She was prepared to feel a sisterly glory in a fame which was to transcend all living literary fame that had gone before it in Great Britain. She had written to him in prospect of his visit to London in March, 1815, in the midst of the excitement produced by the news of Bonaparte's escape from Elba. "Thank Heaven you are coming at last. Make up your mind to be stared at only a little less than the Czar of Moscow or old Blucher." The reception accorded to the author of "Marmion" six years before, was brilliant, but ten times more brilliant was that given to the reputed author of "Waverley." Princes came forward to do him honour. He was presented at the Prince Regent's levee, dined at Carlton House, and received from his future king a gold snuff-box, in token of regard. The snuff-box was set in brilliants, and had a medallion of his Royal Highness's head on the lid.

Sir Walter was accompanied, as before, by Mrs. Scott and his daughter Sophia. He and his wife again stayed with the Dumergues, in Piccadilly; and Sophia, a girl of sixteen, too delicate a blossom for the late hours and the hot rooms of London, was sent out, as formerly, to the maidenly home at Hampstead. She was musically gifted, and was old enough to while their hearts and ears by singing to them and their evening visitors her father's favourite ballads, "Kenmure's on and awa, Willie," and "A weary lot is thine, fair maid," or blithe, unpublished songs—Miss Joanna's own—"Saw ye Johnnie comin', quo' she?" and "Wooed an' married an' a'."

During his stay in London, Sir Walter met Lord Byron, and became on cordial terms with him. Lady Byron, who was then with her husband, pining in his shadow, had been Joanna's dear young friend, and Lord Byron was her personal acquaintance. She recalled the unhappy couple long afterwards.

> "I see her mated with a moody lord,
> Whose fame she prized, whose genius she adored.
> There by his side she stands, pale, grave, and sad,
> The brightness of her greeting smile is fled.
> Like some fair flower ta'en from its genial mould
> To deck a garden-border loose and cold,
> Its former kindred fences all destroyed,
> Shook by the breeze, and by the rake annoy'd,
> She seemed, alas! I looked and looked again,
> Tracing the sweet but alter'd face in vain."

Joanna Baillie's play of *The Family Legend* was acted at the new Drury Lane Theatre in the course of Sir Walter's stay in town. She was persuaded to go with him, Mrs. Scott, and Lord Byron, to witness the representation. Her power of self-control could stand her in good stead, and she was well supported. Elizabeth Hamilton had said, on first coming to Edinburgh, that she had seen more men and women of genius standing up in one quadrille than could be found throughout the rest of Europe. The same might have been said of one box in Drury Lane, that night. Yet how few of the simple, honest playgoers guessed that to the slightly rigid little figure of the ageing woman in sober-hued silk, and delicate lace, seated in one of the boxes above them, they owed the heroic sentiments and thrilling situations at which they clapped their hands. Mary Berry saw the performance from Lady Hardwicke's box, either on that evening or on another of the same week. The piece was played for Mr. Bentley's benefit. Mary Berry's opinion was that it could not have been worse acted. Yet she regarded the representation as to some extent a success, and recorded that the fine lines, spoilt though they were, certainly were appreciated and applauded by the pit. Such appreciation and applause must have moved Joanna more than the tribute of the great men who sat beside her, for it was her cherished wish—fated to be baffled—that she should help to raise the stage, and with it the masses who sought from it excitement and entertainment.

Sir Walter did not revisit London, when he hurried to see the battle-field of Waterloo. He sailed from Harwich, and wrote to Joanna, instead of to Paul's kinsfolk, from Paris, giving statistics of the battle, the allied army, and the French capital. But he saw her on his return, when he could speak of nothing but Waterloo.

From 1815 to 1820 were quiet years in Joanna Baillie's life. It really seemed as if she meant to keep her word, and write no more. In 1815 or 1816, while her friends the Berrys were in Paris, she took a trip to France with the rest of the English world who rushed to see the lares and penates of their enemy; but neither Versailles nor Fontainebleau inspired her. She was resting on her laurels, let the *Edinburgh Review* say what it liked, and enjoying her friend's laurels, especially those fresh ones gathered by her great countryman in "Rob Roy," the "Heart of Midlothian," the "Bride of Lammermoor," and "Ivanhoe." Engrossed by work, and half worshipped as he was, he did not forget her. He sent her a boyishly joyous description of "Joanna's Bower" (it must have reminded her of her Gloucestershire friends with their "Justina's Quarry"), which he had planned out of an old gravel pit in his grounds, and had planted with the pinasters that she had sent him. He wrote expressly to tell her how glad he had been to receive poor Lady Byron, and how much he admired and was touched by the forlorn wife. There was a constant interchange of friendly tokens between Hampstead and Abbotsford, from purses and pinasters to grouse and Glenlivat.

In 1817 the polished, accomplished gentleman whose love had cost him his inheritance, and who is remembered as the father of Mary and Agnes Berry, died at Geneva. Joanna, who had last seen him in Paris, wrote to his daughter Mary a long sympathetic letter, lamenting the friend who had always been kind to Joanna. Within a few years she herself was to need the same sympathy in a more unlooked for, and more trying parting.

In 1828 Sir Walter was up in London receiving his baronetcy, and was in a great hurry to get back to Edinburgh before the month of April was ended. The marriage of his daughter Sophia, grown, as her father loved to call her, "a bonnie lass," and a very gentle one, to John Lockhart, in the promise of his youth, was to be celebrated ere May should bring its evil omen. One Sunday Sir Walter spared to Hampstead, Joanna Baillie, and Johnnie Richardson, carrying out with him his "long cornet," young Walter Scott. And doubtless, among Sir Walter's many lady friends to whom he told with characteristic grace "the old, old story" of his young lovers, there were none who would be more interested than the friends—old ones then, who had taken charge once and again of young Sophia Scott, to note her growth, and speculate on her fortunes. Very likely it was on that April Sunday at Hampstead that Sir Walter got Joanna and Agnes Baillie to fix on going down to Scotland that summer once more, because Joanna, the younger, was already fifty-seven, and age, with its disinclination to move from the chimney-corner, its timidity, and its helplessness, was looming at no remote distance.

Therefore, in 1820, Joanna and her sister were again in Scotland. They were in the West, where they saw their old friends, without remarking in them the gulf between the past and the present which had struck the Baillies on their former visit. They were in Edinburgh, where Joanna at last consented to be introduced to Jeffrey, and when the author and the reviewer agreed to "let byganes be byganes." The two were older now, and one of them had had time to become more temperate in her earnestness, without making a compromise of principles, or even of theories. When advancing life called a truce between the foes, they were both great enough to sink all personal offences and meet as friends. And very good friends the rigid opponents proved. Jeffrey never visited London latterly without going out to Hampstead to taste the hospitality, and be enlivened by the conversation, of Joanna Baillie.

On this sojourn in Edinburgh, Joanna witnessed a second time a representation of one of her plays. In this instance, there was an overflowing house. Her person was widely known, and her presence roused alike actors and spectators to the height of enthusiasm. The resounding plaudits were a national offering laid at the feet of Joanna. Gratefully, and with noble simplicity, as she received the demonstration, it had this qualification, that it was only after the play had been changed to a melodrama, and with the spur lent to the audience by their knowledge of the author, that her tragedy of *Constantine* could thus inspire an assembly.

Above all, Joanna visited Abbotsford, where Gustavus, Prince Royal of Sweden, and Prince Leopold, had been before her. Sir Walter and Tom Purdie were alike in their glory, and no cloud the size of a man's hand had yet risen on the broad blue horizon. Lockhart and his wife were prolonging their wedding festivities in the Forest. Strangers more or less brilliant and famous, from all circles and regions, including the farther side of the Atlantic, were "turning" up every day, sending in their cards and letters of introduction, and being liberally entertained by Sir Walter. The old families of Yair, Elibank, and Gala, were making much of their Sheriff's holidays, and hugging him to their heart. The Kelso races and the Jedburgh ball were still "life" and "the world." Sir William Allan, Sir Humphry Davy, old Henry Mackenzie, were to be seen in one group. Sibyl Grey and Maida were among the dumb animals, and the Abbotsford Hunt (a coursing match) and the Abbotsford Kirn were among the entertainments. The scenery was that of the "sillar Tweed," "fair Melrose," and the Eildon hills. In the absence of journal or letters on Joanna's side, or of any incidental notice in Sir Walter's Life, there is no particular record of those swiftly passing days. But surely Joanna was taken not to Ashiestiel alone, but to "lone St. Mary's," to Carterhaugh, with its bloom of blue bells, and to grey Dryburgh; there would be long chats in the library, toasts at the dinner-table, and songs to the harp in the drawing-room, commemorating a period which was unapproachable to three or four of those present at Abbotsford.

As if the sight of her native country had stirred the gift that was in her, Joanna, on her return home, wrote her "Metrical Legends." In them, she went back to the traditions of her youth, and made her far-away ancestor and ancestress, Wallace and Lady Grisel Baillie, her chief hero and chief heroine. This book was brought out in 1821. The same year *De Montfort* was revived at Drury Lane, this time by Edmund Kean, but without any greater success in securing the public ear and voice.

The year 1821, also, brought the death of Joanna's aunt, Mrs. John Hunter, so long a graceful leader of intellectual fashion.

During the dog-days, Sir Walter is found writing to Joanna, that Mackay is going up to London, to play Baillie Nicol Jarvie for a single night at Covent Garden. He begs her and Mrs. Agnes, "of all dear loves," to go and see the character in its inimitable personification, to collect a party of Scotch friends (as he had written Sotheby to do), that they might have the treat, "and so let it not be said that a dramatic genius of Scotland wanted the countenance and protection of Joanna Baillie."

In a postscript to the letter quoted, Sir Walter entreats Joanna to read, and have Mrs. Agnes read to her (alluding to a practice of the sisters), Galt's "Annals of the Parish," "a most excellent novel, if it can be called so."

In 1822, Joanna's attention was often called to Edinburgh, which was in a state of mad excitement at the proposed visit of George IV. Never king had such a master of the ceremonies, since Rubens' health failed at the last moment, and prevented him from conducting the Cardinal Infant through Antwerp. In the meantime Joanna was busy collecting "Poems, chiefly Manuscript, and from living authors; edited, for the benefit of a Friend, by Joanna Baillie," which were to be printed and sold by subscription. A family, intimate in the sisterly house at Hampstead, had fallen into misfortune, and on their behalf Joanna gathered these crumbs from literary tables. She gave original pieces of her own, of Mrs. Hemans', and of Mrs. John Hunter's.

She begged the same from Sir Walter Scott, and Miss Catherine Fanshaw, whose refined and arch humour made so deep an impression on her contemporaries. Joanna had the great satisfaction, very unusual under the circumstances, of raising by her efforts a sum which secured a small competence for her friends.

About this time the Baillies' neighbour, Mr. Richardson, was down buying an estate on Tweedside. Sir Walter heard all the news of Hampstead from him, and sent back with him a bottle of old whisky, accompanied with the assertion that if Joanna would drink enough of it, she would forgive him all his later offences as a correspondent. Sir Walter's letters began to come more sparely, though they were delightful as ever when they did come. They were still genial and fresh, even after the writer had been caught in the toils, and was struggling manfully in the unequal battle to redeem the fortunes which had once promised so splendidly. Now they were describing his visit to Ireland, and the perfect reception which he had met with from his and Joanna's dear friend, Maria Edgeworth.

Again they dwelt on whatever book or public affair was occupying him at the time. Always they detailed home news—of the "long Cornet's" marriage, of Sophia's baby—all the incidents that were happening in the histories of those "honest lads and bonnie lasses, maids, matrons, and bachelors bluff,"—including "little John Hugh, or, as he is popularly styled, Hugh Little John," in whom his grandfather so delighted,—who, like Sir Walter's father's large but short-lived family, were nearly all of them destined to pass away—

"Like snaw-wreaths in thaw,"

long before the elderly woman, Sir Walter's contemporary, to whom he described their starting in life.

In 1823, Joanna and Agnes Baillie were bereaved indeed by the death of their brother, Matthew. He died before he reached old age, at his seat in Gloucestershire. Joanna, a worn and grey-haired woman, in her sixtieth year, was summoned to his side, and beheld the breaking up of his constitution with the deepest grief. Among his nearest and dearest she waited on him, as she had waited on her mother, day and night, supporting all around her by her mingled firmness and tenderness. The public sorrow on the occasion of Dr. Baillie's death had a healing balm for his afflicted family. The thought of the tablet to his memory in Westminster Abbey, put there by his medical brethren, was more cherished by Joanna than any expectation of monumental honour for herself. She wrote to announce the sad event to Sir Walter Scott. He replied in a reverent, gentle, pitying letter of condolence, recording his friendship for the dead, and pointing to another state of existence as a cure for unavailing sorrow. He reminded her, "You are a family of love; though one breach has been made among you, you will only extend your arms towards each other the more, to hide, though you cannot fill up, the gap which has been made."

Every-day life abounds in pathetic contrasts. This year George Thomson, the friend of Burns, republished his "Melodies of Scotland." He included in the book many of Joanna Baillie's "heartsome" fire-side songs, paraphrases of

ditties of the familiar olden time, such as
Matthew Baillie might have hummed and
whistled when he was a "bauld laddie" at
Bothwell or Hamilton schools, and Joanna was
a morsel of mischief in hood and "doddy
mittens," climbing, not the hill of fame, but
outside stairs and garden walls.

Solemnised by the blow which had robbed
life of half its ties and joys, Joanna occupied
herself soon afterwards with a drama, which
was full of her deep religious feeling. This
play, *The Martyr*, was not brought out till
1826. Sir Alexander Johnston, Chief Justice of
Ceylon, believing that it might have a beneficial
effect on the natives under his government, procured its translation into the Cingalese, as well
as that of *The Bride*, a companion drama, which
he had requested from Joanna for the same
purpose. Whether the morals of the natives of
Ceylon were improved by the dramas, or whether,
indeed, the attempt was brought to completion,
is uncertain; but the thought was praiseworthy,
and must have been acceptable to Joanna.

In 1826 came the great crash of the house of

Constable, in which Sir Walter was fatally involved. The hopeless decline of Johnnie Lockhart followed; and, in the spring of the same year, Sir Walter's wife, who had been his partner for twenty-nine years, passed away. These were griefs which Joanna Baillie shared, though the ready pen of her friend staggered and stopped short in conveying tidings of the misery of that time to Hampstead. In the autumn of that year, Sir Walter and his daughter Anne were with the Lockharts in Pall Mall. Sir Walter was on his way to France, to authenticate his materials for the Life of Bonaparte. There was a wide difference between this visit and the Author of "Waverley's" gala reception in 1815. Still, Sir Walter continued able for company, and could even enjoy it. In his journal of the 15th of November, he notes with satisfaction: "At dinner we had a little blow-out on Sophia's part. Lord Dudley, Mr. Hay, Under-Secretary of State, Sir Thomas Lawrence, and Mistress (as she now calls herself) Joanna Baillie and her sister came in the evening. The whole went off pleasantly."

In 1828, Joanna received, in place of Mary Berry's manuscripts, Mary Berry's books—"The Life of Rachel Lady Russell," and the "Comparative View of Social Life in France and England." Joanna's criticism on the last is very characteristic. After praising highly its clear and scholarly style, its liberality and rectitude, she goes on to say that for her part she would have liked the book better had Mary given the world less of court anecdote and more of illustration of the manners of the middling classes of society. There was another thing of which Joanna disapproved—the account given of Voltaire's mistress, Madame de Charte. She urged also that the mention made of the piece of malice perpetrated by Lady Mary Wortley Montague on the disagreeable adventure of Lady Murray, was an offence to that delicacy which was expected in the writings of a woman. Joanna said she honestly pointed out these blemishes, because they had been felt by others whose judgment and feelings she respected, although the generality of readers might not see them in the same light, because Mary Berry had desired to hear her sincere opinion, and because the work itself had sufficient merit to afford such exceptions to its praise.

Mary Berry's answer is equally characteristic. She expressed herself flattered by Joanna's praise, and almost as much by her blame. Had she proposed writing a comparative view of *manners* instead of "social life" she would have found, and so would Joanna, that the *manners* of the "middling classes of society" in both countries were always a bad imitation of the upper. As to the charge of "offending the delicacy which is expected in the writings of a woman," Mary Berry had chiefly to say that if women treat of human nature and human life in history and not in fiction (which, perhaps, they had better not do), human nature and human life are often indelicate; and if such passages in them are treated always with the gravity and the reprobation they deserve, it is all a sensible woman can do, and, as she is not writing for children, all that she can think necessary.

Notwithstanding such differences of opinion

between Joanna Baillie and Mary Berry, their friendship wore well, and was renewed personally in the intervals between Miss Berry's foreign tours. According to these very letters —portions of which have been given—Mary Berry had just been to Hampstead and had missed Joanna, to the regret of the latter, who had gone up to town to remain at her sister-in-law's in Cavendish Square during some days, for the better opportunity of meeting Sir Walter and his daughter, again living with the Lockharts in Pall Mall.

Overwork, anxiety, and family affliction were telling plainly on Sir Walter, when Joanna saw him at the London dinner parties on two successive days, which were interludes in her country life. Sir Walter also went out and breakfasted with her at Hampstead. He thus refers to the visit in his diary—" Found that gifted person extremely well and in the possession of all her native character and benevolence. I would give as much to have a capital picture of her as for any portrait in the world."

So far as word painting can go, a charming

portrait of Joanna Baillie, dating from not many years after this period, has been very kindly and courteously granted to this book by one of Joanna's few distinguished contemporaries who survive—one whose name will remain a household word among us, Harriet Martineau. "A sweeter picture of old age was never seen. Her figure was small, light, and active; her countenance, in its expression of serenity, harmonised wonderfully with her gay conversation and her cheerful voice. Her eyes were beautiful, dark, bright, and penetrating, with the full, innocent gaze of childhood. Her face was altogether comely, and her dress did justice to it. She wore her own silvery hair and a mob cap, with its delicate lace border fitting close round her face. She was well-dressed in handsome dark silks, and her lace caps and collars looked always new. No Quaker ever was neater, while she kept up with the times in her dress as in her habit of mind, as far as became her years. In her whole appearance there was always something for even the passing stranger to admire, and never anything for

the most familiar friend to wish otherwise."
Add to this graphic description Lucy Aikin's
delicate touch—"No one would ever have
taken her for a married woman. An innocent
and maiden grace still hovered over her to the
end of her old age. It was one of her peculiar
charms, and often brought to my mind the line
addressed to the vowed Isabella in *Measure
for Measure*—

 'I hold you for a thing ensky'd and sainty,'"—

and surely the portrait is complete. It would
seem, indeed, that Joanna, though she accuses
herself in one of her letters to Mary Berry of
gathering thorns to sit upon them, and fears that
she is "ower auld to mend," increased in depth
of serenity and in brightness of cheerfulness as
she advanced in age. It might well be the
reward of her truly noble and gentle career,
though some heavy losses and baffling disap-
pointments had befallen her. In the process
the strong, generous wine of her nature had
been mellowed, and every harsh outline in her
character had been softened.

 Their opportunities of meeting in 1828 were

apparently the last which Joanna had of holding intercourse with her dear friend, Sir Walter Scott. If she saw him again after he was a stricken and dying man, when he had advanced so far as London on his continental journey, no memorandum of the circumstance has been preserved, unless among her own papers.

In the summer of 1828 Joanna was with her sister for some time in Devonshire. A passage in a letter to Mary Berry, written nearly ten years later, gives an idea of how much the Baillies had been pleased with the places they saw and the friends they made there. "I should have liked very much to have seen Mrs. Banister," wrote Joanna, in allusion to a Devonshire friend. "I am pleased that she has anything in her house to put her in mind of me. I cannot recall her neat, pretty house, and all the fair country in her neighbourhood, without having a shade of melancholy pass across my mind."

In 1831, Joanna gave publicity to her religious opinions, which, in one mystery of the Christian faith, coincided with those of Milton. Her essay was named "A View of the General Tenor of the New Testament regarding the Nature and Dignity of Jesus Christ." Apart from any peculiarity in her religious creed, Joanna had always been a godly woman in the simplest and best sense of the term. Her remarkable integrity and truthfulness, the meekness to which she had subdued a temper naturally vehement and impatient, and her careful fulfilment of all obligations, were the fruits of her principles. If anything was at first wanting of mercy and pity for the shortcomings of weakness and error, the grace vouchsafed to the grateful experience of her long and earnest life, supplied the deficiency. She had "a constant sense of the unseen, a constant looking forward to the realisation of eternal verities." Her religious convictions had not become less binding with years; on the contrary, she considered that years gave her a title to utter her convictions. Her book, with the peculiarity of faith which it contained, awakened some opposition and caused some offence, which she wistfully deprecated in a letter sent to Mary

Berry on the second edition of the essay being published. Her tone is altered since she fought for her dramatic theory with Jeffrey; moderation is lent to it by the sacredness of the subject as well as by the old heart grown

"Subdued and slow."

"I thank you and Mrs. Somerville for the friendly interest you take in me, which makes you regret my 'coming forward as a sectarian.' This expression struck me, for I consider myself as less of a sectarian than almost any one whom I am acquainted with. I have endeavoured to set in array, for the use of common readers, all the texts of the New Testament bearing upon a certain point of faith, leaving every one to judge for himself from the general tenor of the whole. . . . We have very High Church people here, Calvinists and Evangelists also; but I have never heard that any one of them ever *said* one unkind thing regarding me, and I am sure they have never *done* one."

In 1832, all England — nay, all Europe — lamented the death of Sir Walter Scott, after so rapid an overthrow of bodily and mental vigour that the death seemed untimely. None lamented him more truly than Joanna Baillie.

In 1836, when Joanna was seventy-four, she was forced to relinquish the last expectation of seeing her plays become well-worked stage property. Accordingly, she published a complete edition of her dramas, including, among others not before published, three additional plays on the passions,—*Romiero*, a tragedy; *The Alienated Manor*, a comedy; and *Henriquez*, a tragedy,—with jealousy and remorse for their themes. She had intended that what were new of these later plays should be first published after her death, and then offered for representation to the smaller theatres; but not auguring favourably of the prospects of the stage, she determined to publish these remaining plays, desiring to round off her original design at once. In her preface, she refers pathetically to the reduced ranks of the friends who were left to hail the last of the dramas, the first of which they had welcomed with so much sympathy. But if Death had robbed her of many friends, she had at least lived to disarm one foe. In the *Edinburgh Review* for 1836, appeared a highly appreciative and laudatory article on the collected edition of the plays, with special reference to those which were new to the public. The writer still condemned the plan of the series, and reckoned several of the plays decidedly below the level of the others; but, contemplating Joanna Baillie's finished work as a whole, with respect to the success attained and the difficulties combated, he fairly and honourably admitted that he had altered his opinion. No longer comparing her to the dramatists of the reigns of Elizabeth and James, but matching her with her contemporaries, he frankly owned her superiority to Byron and Scott as dramatists.

Then followed a generous and admiring analysis of Joanna Baillie's plays, with ample quotations from scenes and passages of singular power, tenderness, and grace.

After the article in the *Edinburgh Review* was written, but before it was published, a grand effort was made to establish Joanna's plays on the English stage. Two of them, *Henri-*

quez and *The Separation*, were brought out simultaneously at Covent Garden and Drury Lane. One of the Kembles survived to lend his aid to the part of Garcia, and Mr. Vandenhoff supported that of Henriquez; but the verdict of the mass of playgoers was unreversed. The reviewer could only add to his article a note to the effect—"Nothing has led us so completely to despair of the revival of true dramatic taste among us as the announcement we have just noticed in a newspaper, that *Henriquez*, when represented before a London audience, had been treated, like its predecessors, with comparative coldness; and that its announcement for repetition had been received with some tokens of disapprobation."

In a letter to Mary Berry, of May, 1836, Joanna mentions having been in town, where she dined out twice, and went to Drury Lane to see Mrs. Bartley in Lady Macbeth. She said these were great exertions for her, as they certainly were, even for a light and active old lady of seventy-five years. She adds, with a pardonable inclination to divide at least the causes of failure, "I thought, while in town, I might have got some information that might have enabled me to answer your query—'What has become of *Henriquez?*' but I could learn nothing. I dare say there has been some quarrelling in the green-room about it, and that the actors have not liked their parts, though the piece was so favourably received by a very full house. However this may be, I don't expect it to be produced in Drury Lane again." Then she drops the subject, and proceeds to describe Lady Byron's school for boys of the common ranks at Ealing, a pioneer industrial school. Joanna admired the arrangement by which the boys were instructed in trades while they received ordinary education; and prophesied that the boys would be especially qualified for new settlers in the colonies; verifying the prediction by the statement that the carpenters and the gardeners of Acton and Ealing were "mighty glad to have the boys for apprentices."

The play of *Romiero* met with considerable general criticism, on the ground that its expression of jealousy was inconsistent with the interest and the dignity of tragedy. Joanna had still sufficient spirit to defend her play from these strictures in *Fraser's Magazine* for December, 1836.

If it could be any consolation to Joanna for this comparative failure as a dramatist, her fame was great in America. She (as well as her friend Lucy Aikin) was in frequent correspondence with Dr. Channing. Beyond the Atlantic, she had many other distinguished correspondents, who occasionally sent representatives to knock at her readily-opened door at Hampstead. She even received a diploma, constituting her a member of the Michigan Historical Society, and declared herself proud of the compliment.

In 1837, Joanna wrote to Mary Berry, who was only one year younger—"May God support both you and me, and give us comfort and consolation when it is most wanted. As for myself, I do not wish to be one year younger than I am, and have no desire, were it possible, to begin life again, even under the most honourable circumstances. I have great cause for humble thankfulness, and I am thankful."

In 1840, Lord Jeffrey, an ageing, failing man himself, was in England, and recorded of his ancient antagonist:—"I have been twice out to Hampstead and found Joanna Baillie as fresh, natural, and amiable as ever, and as little like a tragic muse." In 1842 he again wrote of her—"She is marvellous in health and spirits; not a bit deaf, blind, or torpid." And this was when Joanna had reached that term of four-score which, when attained, is so often "but labour and sorrow."

It was about this time that Joanna published her last book. It was of a different order from the others, being a volume of "Fugitive Verses," republished from her early poems of nearly fifty years before, together with some songs published for the first time. These verses were for the most part simple lyrics on domestic anniversaries, and addressed to private friends. She stated in the preface that she had been induced to bring out this last volume, partly in consequence of discovering that some of her scattered pieces had been extracted and preserved by judges whom she esteemed, and partly in consequence of the warmly-expressed opinion in favour of her early and neglected poems which had been given by her friend, Samuel Rogers. She commented on the period at which most of the verses were written. Miss Seward, Hayley, and Burns (who was hardly known in England) were then the poets spoken of in literary circles as affording models for poetic composition; and she bespoke the world's indulgence for her lyrics rather on the ground of their being a homely, refreshing variety than on any other. She explained, in order to avoid the imputation of forwardness or presumption, that the psalms marked "for the Kirk," were written at the request of an eminent member of the Scotch Church, at a time when a new collection of hymns was contemplated for the use of parochial congregations. She declared that it would have gratified her extremely to have been of the smallest service to the venerable Church of her native land, "which the conscientious zeal of the great majority of an intelligent and virtuous nation had founded;

which their unconquerable courage, endurance of persecution, and unwearied perseverance, had reared into a Church as effective for private virtue and ecclesiastical government as any Protestant establishment in Europe." She was proud to be so occupied; her heart and her duty went along with the occupation; but the General Assembly refused their sanction to the measure. The daughter of the former minister of Bothwell and Hamilton vindicated loyally the decision of the Assembly, which rendered useless what she and "far better poets" had written for the purpose. She urged it as a circumstance at which we ought not to be surprised, "that clergymen who had been accustomed from their youth to hear the noble Psalms of David sung by the mingled voices of a large congregation, swelling often to a sublime volume of sound, elevating the mind and quickening the feelings beyond all studied excitement of art, should regard any additions or changes as presumptuous."

In the lines addressed to her sister, Joanna gives a very graceful and tender picture of the two women in their peaceful home, occupied with the pursuits of their genial old age.

"Let what will engage
Thy present moment, whether hopeful seeds
In garden-plot thou sow, or noxious weeds
From the fair flower remove, or ancient lore
In chronicle or legend rare explore,
Or on the parlour hearth with kitten play,
Stroking its tabby sides, or take thy way
To gain with hasty steps some cottage door,
On helpful errand to the neighbouring poor,
Active and ardent to my fancy's eye,
Thou still art young, in spite of time gone by.
Though oft of patience brief, and temper keen,
Well may it please me, in life's latter scene,
To think what now thou art and long to me hast been.

  * * * *

And now, in later years, with better grace,
Thou help'st me still to hold a welcome place
With those whom nearer neighbourhood has made
The friendly cheerers of our evening shade.
With thee my humours, whether grave or gay,
Or gracious or untoward, have their way—
Silent if dull—O precious privilege!
I sit by thee; or if, call'd from the page
Of some huge ponderous tome, which, but thyself,
None e'er had taken from its dusty shelf,
Thou read me curious passages, to speed
The winter night, I take but little heed,
And thankless say, 'I cannot listen now,'
'Tis no offence; albeit much do I owe
To these, thy nightly offerings of affection,
Drawn from thy ready talent for selection;
For still it seemed in thee a natural gift,
The letter'd grain from letter'd chaff to sift.

By daily use and circumstance endear'd,
Things are of value now that once appear'd
Of no account, and without notice past,
Which o'er dull life a simple cheering cast;
To hear thy morning step the stairs descending,
Thy voice with other sounds domestic blending;
After each stated nightly absence met,
To see thee by the morning table set,
Pouring from smoky spout the amber stream,
Which sends from saucer'd cup its fragrant steam;
To see thee cheerly on the threshold stand,
On summer morn, with trowel in thy hand,
For garden work prepared; in winter's gloom
From thy cold noonday walk to see thee come,
In furry garment lapp'd, with spatter'd feet,
And by the fire resume thy wonted seat;
Ay, even o'er things like these sooth'd age has thrown
A sober charm they did not always own,
As winter hoar-frost makes minutest spray
Of bush or hedge-weed sparkle to the day
In magnitude and beauty, which bereaved
Of such investment, eye had ne'er perceived.
The change of good and evil to abide,
As partners linked, long have we side by side
Our earthly journey held; and who can say
How near the end of our united way?
By nature's course not distant: sad and reft
Will she remain,—the lonely pilgrim left.
If thou be taken first, who can to me
Like sister, friend, and home-companion be?
Or who, of wonted daily kindness shorn,
Shall feel such loss, and mourn as I shall mourn?

> And if I should be fated first to leave
> This earthly house, though gentle friends may grieve,
> And above them all, so truly proved
> A friend and brother long and justly loved,
> There is no living wight of woman born
> Who then shall mourn for me as thou wilt mourn."

But the young life of kindred descendants, with its gladsome stir, was not absent from the Baillies' house. Joanna's loving, overflowing lines "To an Infant," to "Sophia J. Baillie," to "Two Brothers," to "James B. Baillie," show how closely the thoughts of niece and grand-nephew were entwined round her heart. Of one of them she wrote:—

> "Yes, Heaven perhaps thine aged aunt may spare
> Some years in these thy childhood's beams to share:
> Thy fair beginning may her ending cheer,
> But aught beyond will not to her appear.
> And when to man's estate thou dost attain
> No trace of her will in thy mind remain.
> Ay, so it needs must be, and be it so,
> Though ne'er for thee will heart more warmly glow."

In 1844, Joanna, acknowledging Mary Berry's promised gift of a new and complete edition of all her *brochures*, reflected a little sadly, "If I were much given to envy, I should envy you for two things: first, that a clever, knowing-in-the-trade bookseller calls for permission to reprint your works; and, next, that you can still read with undivided attention, and take an interest in every subject before you. On what spot of the earth lives that bookseller who would now publish at his own risk any part of my works? And what book could you give me to read of which I should have any distinct recollection three months hence?"

With regard to the first question, Joanna lived to see another publication of her whole works in a collected form, made seven years afterwards, and only a few weeks before her death. Mary Berry answered the question more rapidly, in a frank and kind protest. "Why, what a goose you are!—(that ever I, M. B., should dare to call Joanna Baillie a goose). But don't you see that 'a clever, knowing-in-the-trade bookseller' reprints trifles made for a drawing-room table and the talk of the day, and not works written for posterity, and to take their place in the small band of real poets who have adorned our country? *There* you will flourish ever green, and will rise in importance as you recede from the present generation; *there* Shakspeare will acknowledge that you dared walk on the same plank with him, without copying him, or falling from the height of which he had shown you the example; *there* Byron will own that your expression of passion in *Basil* exceeds any of his, although calling to his aid sentiment and scenes drawn from that vicious circle to which you disdained having recurrence, and into whose precincts your muse never wandered."

These letters seem to have been the last which passed between the old friends. In the end of her letter Joanna's spirit brightens into something beyond resignation. After remarking that they two still looked forward to months and half-years, as they formerly did to longer periods, willing to remain as long as their Heavenly Father pleased they should, and no longer, she adds, "For me, the walking through our churchyard is no unpleasant thing; it cannot extinguish the lights beaming from the promised house in which are many mansions."

Mary Berry thus closes her share of the correspondence, "And now, my dear Joanna, God bless you! .... Once more, God bless you!"

Joanna Baillie lived, as has been said, some years longer, leading always a more secluded and peaceful life. At last on Sunday, the 23rd of February, 1851, when she had entered her ninetieth year, not more than twenty-four hours from the time when she had expressed a strong desire to be released from life, she passed away "without suffering, in the full possession of her faculties, with sorrowing relations around her, in the act of devotion." Mary Russel Mitford mentions that in a letter from Joanna Baillie to a friend, written a very few days before her death, she expressed her satisfaction in having received the sacrament along with her sister on the previous Sunday. Mary and Agnes Berry died the following year. Lucy Aikin, Joanna's intimate friend for half a century, died three years after Joanna Baillie, and was buried in the grave next to her whom she had loved and honoured, in the old churchyard at Hampstead. There was space on the other side for Agnes, the fond and faithful sister, who nearly attained the full round of a century.

Of Joanna Baillie's plays it is not necessary to say anything. The best judges have long ago dissected and analysed them, and agreed as to their amount of merit. If she was tempted to generalise, it was because of a breadth of mind which was very extraordinary in a woman. If the well-balanced character of that mind gave her a preference for well-balanced, somewhat monotonous characters, notwithstanding that her aim was a delineation of the passions, it saved her grasp of comprehension from ever becoming spasmodic. Her female characters and her softer scenes had no want of throbbing sensibility and gentle grace. The independence and touch of wrong-headedness which prevented her from being guided and influenced by more experienced, better informed people, were but the effects (unfortunate, if you will) of her native freshness and determination of mind; and possibly she paid a heavy price for them in the dragging construction, which, as a rule, shut out her plays from the stage.

Joanna Baillie's "Fugitive Verses" were, like her plays, unequal; but they vindicated her excellence in affectionate and playful composition. Her "Kitten," and "A Child to his Sick Grandfather," are very happy instances. Many of Joanna Baillie's songs are simply exquisite in their tripping measure, fine taste, concentrated feeling, and beautiful imagery. Her Scotch songs are much more than happy. They show, on a small scale, the mingled breadth and delicacy of handling seen in her plays. Every element of interest is treated as it deserves. Each is in due subordination, while the treatment is eloquent, racy, full of humour, and of kindly affection. So sunny are these songs, and at the same time so ripe in their colouring, that one ceases to wonder at her statement which at first provoked Sir Walter Scott's laughter, that she could not write her lyrics save on a warm day. One peculiarity remains about them. Although she made love the master-passion in Count Basil, and her severest critics did not accuse her of any incapacity to enter into the subtle recesses and lay bare the wild vagaries of the passion, there is hardly what can be called a love-song among all she wrote. Not one answers to Susanna Blamire's "What ails this heart o' mine?" Perhaps the nearest to a love-song is "The Shepherd's Watch by the Trysting Bush," with its passion of longing; yet even that is slightly and tenderly, but very plainly, made fun of. Another peculiarity to be noticed is, that, while it is now generally granted that the weak point in Joanna Baillie's work was her comedies, indeed that she could not write a good comedy, still, sufficient for the production of very droll songs were "the placid cheerfulness and gay good sense," "the ease and purity of language," which Jeffrey in his first attack allowed that she possessed, but which he pronounced quite inadequate qualities for the demands of a comedy.

Among the entirely waggish songs, are "Tam o' the Lin," "Hooly and Fairly," new words to the "Weary Pund o' Tow," "The Merry Bachelor," "'Twas on a Morn when we were Thrang," and "Fy, let us a' to the Wedding"—

an admirable paraphrase of the clever but gross song of Semple of Beltrees.

Among those characterised by a modified waggery, and with a substratum of sentiment, are, "Poverty parts good Company," "'Saw ye Johnnie comin'?' quo' she," "The Lover's Watch," the first new set of "The Weary Pund o' Tow," "Wi' Lang-legged Tam the broose I tried," and "Woo'd and Married and a'."

"Oh! swiftly glides the Bonnie Boat," is the only one of Joanna Baillie's Scotch songs about which humour does not glint and play. This song is often confounded with Lady Nairne's version of "The Boatie Rows."

It is next to impossible to individualise excellencies where they are so abundant. The spirit and graphicness of the following verses speak for themselves:—

> "Wi' lang-legg'd Tam the broose I tried,
> Though best o' foot, what wan he O?
> The first kiss o' the blowzy bride,
> But I the heart of Nanny O.
>
> "I'm nearly wild, I'm nearly daft,
> Wad fain be douce, but canna O;
> There's ne'er a laird o' muir or craft,
> Sae blithe as I wi' Nanny O.

> "Her angry mither scaulds sae loud,
> And darkly glooms her granny O;
> But think they he can e'er be cow'd
> Who loves and lives for Nanny O?
>
> "The spae-wife on my loof that blink't
> Is but a leein' ran'y O;
> For weel kens she my fate is link't
> In spite o' a' to Nanny O."

The same glee and spirit are seen in "The Merry Bachelor:"—

> "The bride forgot her simple groom,
> And every lass her trysted jo;
> Yet nae man's brow on Will could gloom,
> They liked his rousing blitheness so.
>
> "The carline left her housewife's wark,
> The bairnies shouted Willie's name,
> The colley too would fidge and bark,
> And wag his tail when Willie came."

How subtly wise and tender are the remonstrances of the father and the mother in "Woo'd and Married and a'!"

> "Her mither then hastily spak:
> 'The lassie is glaikit wi' pride;
> In my pouch I had never a plack
> The day that I was a bride.

> E'en tak' to your wheel and be clever,
>   And draw out your thread in the sun;
> The gear that is gifted, it never
>   Will last like the gear that is won.
>   Woo'd and married and a'!
>   Wi' havins and tocher sae sma'!
>   I think ye are very weel aff
>   To be woo'd and married and a'."
>
> "'Toot, toot!' quo' her grey-headed faither,
>   'She's less o' a bride than a bairn;
> She's ta'en like a cowt frae the heather,
>   Wi' sense and discretion to learn.
> Half husband, I trow, and half daddy,
>   As humour inconstantly leans,
> The chiel maun be patient and steady
>   That yokes wi' a mate in her teens.
>   A kerchief sae douce and sae neat,
>   O'er her locks that the wind used to blaw!
>   I'm baith like to laugh and to greet
>   When I think o' her married at a'.'"

And what a picture of bashful, roguish love, that conquers mortified vanity, is in the conduct of the bride!

> "She turn'd, and she blush'd, and she smiled,
>   And she lookit sae bashfully down;
> The pride o' her heart was beguiled,
>   And she play'd wi' the sleeve o' her gown,
> She twirled the tag o' her lace,
>   And she nippit her boddice sae blue,
> Syne blinkit sae sweet in his face,
>   And aff like a mawkin she flew.

> Woo'd and married and a'!
> Wi' Johnnie to roose her and a'!
> She thinks hersel' very weel aff
> To be woo'd and married and a'."

A nice distinction, as well as "a full and particular account of the whole matter," is contained in the repeated and emphatic statements of another song :—

> "For a chap at the door in braid daylight
> Is no like a chap that is heard at e'en."
>
> "An elderlin man i' the noon o' the day
> Should be wiser than youngsters that come at e'en."

The wife has reached the last extremity in "Hooly and Fairly":—

> "I' the kirk sic commotion last Sabbath she made,
> Wi' babs o' red roses and breast-knots o'erlaid;
> The dominie stickit the psalm very nearly.
> O gin my wife wad dress hooly and fairly!
>   Hooly and fairly, hooly and fairly;
> O gin my wife wad dress hooly and fairly!

And so has the husband with his cry of despair—

> "I wish I were single, I wish I were freed,
> I wish I were doited, I wish I were dead;

> Or she in the mools to dement me nae mairly.
> What does't avail to cry hooly and fairly?
> Hooly and fairly, hooly and fairly;
> Wasting my breath to cry hooly and fairly!"

There is a sweet archness in number one of Joanna Baillie's "Weary Pund o' Tow," and it presents a succession of charming rural scenes. The fire of the lass imaged in number two reminds the reader of the "Miss Jack," who, to the admiration of the old Clydeside farmer, sat her pony as if she were a part of the beast.

The conceit, the imperturbability, the irony of "Tam o' the Lin" are inimitable.

In "'Saw ye Johnnie comin'?' quo' she," the spell woven round the speaker, and the double inducements which she offers, combine to give the song a quaint uniqueness:—

> "'Saw ye Johnnie comin'?' quo' she,
> 'Saw ye Johnnie comin'?
> Wi' his blue bonnet on his head,
> And his doggie runnin'?
> Yestreen, about the gloamin' time,
> I chanced to see him comin',
> Whistling merrily the tune
>   That I am a' day hummin',' quo' she,
>   'I am a' day hummin.'

"'Fee him, faither, fee him,' quo' she;
'Fee him, faither, fee him;
A' the wark about the house
Gaes wi' me when I see him.
A' the wark about the house
I gang sae lightly through it;
And though ye pay some merks o' gear,
Hoot! ye winna rue it,' quo' she,
'Na! ye winna rue it.'

* * * *

"'Weel do I lo'e him,' quo' she,
'Weel do I lo'e him;
The brawest lads about the place
Are a' but haverels to him.
O fee him, faither; lang, I trow,
We've dull and dowie been;
He'll haud the plough, thrash i' the barn,
And crack wi' me at e'en,' quo' she,
'Crack wi' me at e'en.'"

The Scotch song which has least of Joanna's humour, and least nationality, has a melodiousness which harmonises with its subject, and which has insured it popularity.

"O swiftly glides the bonnie boat,
Just parted from the shore,
And to the fisher's chorus note
Soft moves the dipping oar.

* * * *

We cast our lines in Largo Bay,
    Our nets are floating wide;
Our bonnie boat, with lurching sway,
    Rocks lightly on the tide.

   *   *   *   *

"The mermaid on her rock may sing,
    The witch may weave her charm,
Nor water-sprite nor ehritch thing
    The bonnie boat can harm.
It safely bears its scaly store
    Through many a stormy gale,
While joyful shouts rise from the shore,
    Its homeward prow to hail."

WI' LANG-LEGG'D TAM.

Wi' lang-legg'd Tam the broose I tried,
    Though best o' foot, what wan he O?
The first kiss o' the blowzy bride,
    But I the heart of Nanny O.

Like swallow wheeling round her tower,
    Like rock-bird round her cranny O,
Sinsyne I hover near her bower,
    And list and look for Nanny O.

I'm nearly wild, I'm nearly daft,
    Wad fain be douce, but canna O;
There's ne'er a laird o' muir or craft
    Sae blithe as I wi' Nanny O.

She's sweet, she's young, she's fair, she's good,
  The brightest maid of many O.
Though a' the world our love withstood,
  I'd woo and win my Nanny O.

Her angry mither scaulds sae loud,
  And darkly glooms her granny O;
But think they he can e'er be cow'd
  Who loves and lives for Nanny O?

The spae-wife on my loof that blink't
  Is but a leein' rin'y O,
For weel kens she my fate is link't
  In spite o' a' to Nanny O.

THE MERRY BACHELOR.

Willie was a wanton wag,
  The blithest lad that e'er I saw,
Of field and floor he was the brag,
  And carried a' the gree awa'.

And wasna Willie stark and keen
  When he gaed to the wappen-schaw?
He won the prizes on the green,
  And cheer'd the feasters in the ha'.

His head was wise, his heart was leal,
  His truth was fair without a flaw,
And aye by every honest chiel
  His word was holden as a law.

And wasna Willie still our pride,
  When in his gallant gear arrayed,
He wan the broose and kissed the bride,
  While pipes the wedding-welcome played?

And aye he led the foremost dance
  Wi' winsome maidens buskit braw,
And gave to each a merry glance,
  That stole awhile her heart awa'.

The bride forgot her simple groom,
  And every lass her trysted jo;
Yet nae man's brow on Will could gloom,
  They liked his rousing blitheness so.

Our good Mess John laughed wi' the lave;
  The dominie, for a' his lore,
Could scarcely like himself behave,
  While a' was glee and revel there.

A joyous sight was Willie's face,
  Baith far and near in ilka spot;
In ha' received wi' kindly grace,
  And welcomed to the lowly cot.

The carline left her housewife's wark,
    The bairnies shouted Willie's name;
The colley too would fidge and bark,
    And wag his tail when Willie came.

But Willie now has crossed the main,
    And he has been sae lang awa'!
Oh! would he were returned again,
    To drive the dowfness frae us a'.

WOO'D AND MARRIED AND A'.

The bride she is winsome and bonny,
    Her hair it is snooded sae sleek,
And faithfu' and kind is her Johnny,
    Yet fast fa' the tears on her cheek.
New pearlins are cause of her sorrow,
    New pearlins and plenishing too;
The bride that has a' to borrow
    Has e'en right mickle ado.
      Woo'd and married and a'!
      Woo'd and married and a'!
      Isna she very weel aff
      To be woo'd and married and a'?

Her mither then hastily spak:
    "The lassie is glaikit wi' pride;
In my pouch I had never a plack
    The day that I was a bride.

E'en tak' to your wheel and be clever,
  And draw out your thread in the sun;
The gear that is gifted, it never
  Will last like the gear that is won.
    Woo'd and married and a'!
    Wi' havins and tocher sae sma'!
    I think ye are very weel aff
    To be woo'd and married and a'!"

"Toot! toot!" quo' her grey-headed faither,
  "She's less o' a bride than a bairn;
She's ta'en like a cowt frae the heather,
  Wi' sense and discretion to learn.
Half husband, I trow, and half daddy,
  As humour inconstantly leans,
The chiel maun be patient and steady
  That yokes wi' a mate in her teens.
    A kerchief sae douce and sae neat,
    O'er her locks that the wind used to blaw!
    I'm baith like to laugh and to greet
    When I think o' her married at a'!"

Then out spak the wily bridegroom;
  Weel waled were his wordies I ween:
"I'm rich, though my coffer be toom,
  Wi' the blink o' your bonny blue e'en.
I'm prouder o' thee by my side,
  Though thy ruffles and ribbons be few,

Than if Kate o' the Craft were my bride,
  Wi' purples and pearlins enou'.
    Dear and dearest of ony !
    Ye're woo'd and buiket and a' !
    And do ye think scorn o' your Johnny,
    And grieve to be married at a' ?"

She turn'd, and she blush'd, and she smiled,
  And she lookit sae bashfully down ;
The pride o' her heart was beguiled,
  And she play'd wi' the sleeve o' her gown,
She twirled the tag o' her lace,
  And she nippit her boddice sae blue,
Syne blinkit sae sweet in his face,
  And aff like a mawkin she flew.
    Woo'd and married and a' !
    Wi' Johnny to roose her and a' !
    She thinks hersel' very weel aff
    To be woo'd and married and a' !

IT FELL ON A MORN WHEN WE WERE THRANG.

It fell on a morn when we were thrang ;
  The kirn it crooned, the cheese was making,
  And bannocks on the gridle baking,
When ane at the door chapt loud and lang.

Yet the auld gudewife, and her Mays sae tight,
  Of a' this bauld din took sma' notice, I ween,
For a chap at the door in braid daylight
  Is no like a chap that is heard at e'en.

But the clocksy auld laird of the Warlock glen,
  Wha waited without, half blate, half cheery,
And langed for a sight o' his winsome deary,
Raised up the latch, and came crousely ben.
His coat was new, and his o'erlay was white;
  His mittens and hose were cozie and bien;
But a wooer that comes in braid daylight
  Is no like a wooer that comes at e'en.

He greeted the carline and lasses sae braw,
  And his bare lyart pow sae smoothly he straikit,
And lookit about like a body half glaikit
On bonny sweet Nanny, the youngest of a'.
"Ah, laird!" quo' the carline, "and look ye that way?
  Fye, letna sic fancies bewilder you clean;
An elderlin man i' the noon o' the day
  Should be wiser than youngsters that come at e'en."

"Na, na," quo' the pawky auld wife; "I trow
  You'll no fash your head wi' a youthfu' gilly,
As wild and as skeich as a muirland filly;
Black Madge is far better and fitter for you."

He hemm'd and he haw'd, and he drew in his mouth,
  And he squeezed the blue bonnet his twa hands
    between,
For a wooer that comes when the sun's i' the south
  Is mair landward than wooers that come at e'en.

"Black Madge is sae careful——" "What's that to me?"
  "She's sober and eident, has sense in her noddle;
  She's douce and respeckit." "I carena a bodle;
Love winna be guided, and my fancy's free."
Madge toss'd back her head wi' a saucy slight,
  And Nanny, loud laughing, ran out to the green;
For a wooer that comes when the sun shines bright
  Is no like a wooer that comes at e'en.

Then awa' flung the laird, and loud muttered he:
  "A' the daughters of Eve, between Orkney and
    Tweed O!
  Black or fair, young or auld, dame or damsel or widow,
May gang wi' their pride to the deil for me!"
But the auld gudewife, and her Mays sae tight,
  Cared little for a' his stour banning, I ween;
For a wooer that comes in braid daylight
  Is no like a wooer that comes at e'en.

FY, LET US A' TO THE WEDDING.

Fy, let us a' to the wedding,
    For they will be lilting there;
For Jock's to be married to Maggy,
    The lass wi' the gowden hair.

And there will be gibing and jeering,
    And glancing of bonny dark e'en;
Loud laughing and smooth-gabbit speering
    O' questions baith pawky and keen.

And there will be Bessy the beauty,
    Wha raises her cockup sae hie,
And giggles at preachings and duty;
    Gude grant that she gang not agee!

And there will be auld Geordie Tanner,
    Wha coft a young wife wi' his gowd;
She'll flaunt wi' a silk gown upon her,
    But now he looks dowie and cow'd!

And brown Tibby Fowler, the heiress,
    Will poke at the tap o' the ha',
Encircled wi' suitors, wha's care is
    To catch up her gloves when they fa',

Repeat a' her jokes as they're cleckit,
    And haver and glower in her face,

When tocherless Mays are negleckit—
  A' crying, a scandalous case.

And Mysie, wha's clavering aunty
  Wad match her wi' Laurie the Laird,
And learn the young fule to be vaunty,
  But neither to spin nor to card.

And Andrew, wha's granny is yearning
  To see him a clerical blade,
Was sent to the college for learning,
  And came back a coof as he gaed.

And there will be auld Widow Martin,
  That ca's hersel thritty and twa!
And thrawn-gabbit Madge, wha for certain
  Has jilted Hal o' the Shaw.

And Elspy, the swoster sae genty,
  A pattern of havins and sense,
Will straik on her mittens sae dainty,
  And crack wi' Mass John in the spence.

And Angus, the seer o' ferlies,
  That sits on the stane at his door,
And tells about bogles, and mair lees
  Than tongue ever uttered before.

And there will be Bauldy the boaster,
  Sae ready wi' hands and wi' tongue;

Proud Paty and silly Sam Foster,
    Wha quarrel wi' auld and wi' young.

And Hugh, the town-writer, I'm thinking,
    That trades in his lawerly skill,
Will egg on the fighting and drinking,
    To bring after-grist to his mill.

And Maggy—na, na, we'll be civil,
    And let the wee bridie a-be;
A vilipend tongue is the devil,
    And ne'er was encouraged by me.

Then fy, let us a' to the wedding,
    For they will be lilting there,
Frae mony a far-distant haudin',
    The fun and the feasting to share.

For they will get sheep's-head and haggis,
    And browst o' the barley-mow;
E'en he that comes latest and lag is,
    May feast upon dainties enow.

Veal florentins in the o'en bakin',
    Weel plenished wi' raisins and fat;
Beef, mutton, and chuckies all taken
    Het reekin' frae spit and frae pat.

And glasses (I trow 'tis na' said ill),
    To drink the young couple good luck,

Weel filled wi' a braw bucken ladle,
  Frae punch-bowl as big as Dumbuck.

And then will come dancing and daffing,
  And reeling and crossing o' han's,
Till even auld Lucky is laughing,
  As back by the aumry she stan's.

Sic bobbing, and flinging, and whirling,
  While fiddlers are making their din;
And pipers are droning and skirling
  As loud as the roar o' the lin.

Then fy, let us a' to the wedding,
  For they will be lilting there;
For Jock's to be married to Maggy,
  The lass wi' the gowden hair.

HOOLY AND FAIRLY.

Oh, neighbours! what had I ado for to marry?
My wife she drinks possets and wine o' Canary,
And ca's me a niggardly, thrawn-gabbit cairly.
O gin my wife wad drink hooly and fairly!
  Hooly and fairly, hooly and fairly;
O gin my wife wad drink hooly and fairly!

She feasts wi' her kimmers on dainties enew,
Aye bowsing and smirking and wiping her mou',
While I sit aside and am helpit but sparely.
O gin my wife wad feast hooly and fairly !
    Hooly and fairly, hooly and fairly ;
O gin my wife wad feast hooly and fairly !

To fairs and to bridals, and preachings and a',
She gangs sae light-hearted and buskit sae braw,
In ribbons and mantuas that gar me gae barely !
O gin my wife wad spend hooly and fairly !
    Hooly and fairly, hooly and fairly ;
O gin my wife wad spend hooly and fairly !

I' the kirk sic commotion last Sabbath she made,
Wi' babs o' red roses and breast-knots o'erlaid !
The dominie stickit the psalm very nearly.
O gin my wife wad dress hooly and fairly !
    Hooly and fairly, hooly and fairly ;
O gin my wife wad dress hooly and fairly !

She's warring and flyting frae morning till e'en ;
And if ye gainsay her, her e'en glour sae keen;
Then tongue, nieve, and cudgel she'll lay on ye sairly !
O gin my wife wad strike hooly and fairly !
    Hooly and fairly, hooly and fairly ;
O gin my wife wad strike hooly and fairly !

When tired wi' her cantrips she lies in her bed,
The wark a' negleckit, the chaumer unred,
While a' our gude neighbours are stirring sae early.
O gin my wife wad sleep timely and fairly!
　　Timely and fairly, timely and fairly;
O gin my wife wad sleep timely and fairly!

A word o' gude counsel or grace she'll hear none,
She bardies the elders and mocks at Mess John,
While back in his teeth his ain text she flings rarely.
O gin my wife wad speak hooly and fairly!
　　Hooly and fairly, hooly and fairly;
O gin my wife wad speak hooly and fairly!

I wish I were single, I wish I were freed,
I wish I were doited, I wish I were dead,
Or she in the mools to dement me nae mairly!
What does't avail to cry hooly and fairly?
　　Hooly and fairly, hooly and fairly;
Wasting my breath to cry hooly and fairly!

THE WEARY PUND O' TOW.

　A young gudewife is in my house,
　　And thrifty means to be;
　But aye she's runnin' to the town
　　Some ferlie there to see.

The weary pund, the weary pund,
   The weary pund o' tow,
I soothly think ere it be spun
   I'll wear a lyart pow.

And when she sets her to the wheel,
   To draw the threads wi' care,
In comes the chapman wi' his gear,
   And she can spin nae mair.
           The weary pund, &c.

And she, like mony merry May,
   At fairs maun still be seen;
At kirkyard preachings near the tent,
   At dances on the green.
           The weary pund, &c.

Her dainty ear a fiddle charms,
   A bagpipe's her delight;
But for the croonings o' her wheel
   She disna care a mite.
           The weary pund, &c.

You spak, my Kate, of snow-white webs,
   Made o' your linkum-twine,
But ah! I fear our bonny burn
   Will ne'er lave web o' thine.
           The weary pund, &c.

Nay, smile again, my winsome Kate!
Sic jibings mean nae ill;
Should I gae sarkless to my grave,
I'll lo'e and bless thee still.
    The weary pund, &c.

TAM O' THE LIN.

Tam o' the Lin was fu' o' pride,
And his weapon he girt to his valorous side,
A scabbard o' leather wi' de'il-hair't within.
"Attack me wha daur!" quo' Tam o' the Lin.

Tam o' the Lin he bought a mear;
She cost him five shillings, she wasna dear.
Her back stuck up, and her sides fell in.
"A fiery yaud," quo' Tam o' the Lin.

Tam o' the Lin he courted a May;
She stared at him sourly, and said him nay;
But he stroked down his jerkin and cocked up his chin.
"She aims at a laird, then," quo' Tam o' the Lin.

Tam o' the Lin he gaed to the fair,
Yet he looked wi' disdain on the chapman's ware;
Then chucked out a sixpence, the sixpence was tin.
"There's coin for the fiddlers," quo' Tam o' the Lin.

Tam o' the Lin wad show his lear,
And he scanned o'er the book wi' wise-like stare.
He muttered confusedly, but didna begin.
"This is Dominie's business," quo' Tam o' the Lin.

Tam o' the Lin had a cow wi' ae horn,
That likit to feed on his neighbour's corn.
The stanes he threw at her fell short o' the skin;
"She's a lucky auld reiver," quo' Tam o' the Lin.

Tam o' the Lin he married a wife,
And she was the torment, the plague o' his life;
She lays sae about her, and maks sic a din,
"She frightens the baby," quo' Tam o' the Lin.

Tam o' the Lin grew dowie and douce,
And he sat on a stane at the end o' his house.
"What ails, auld chield?" He looked haggard and thin.
"I'm no very cheery," quo' Tam o' the Lin.

Tam o' the Lin lay down to die,
And his friends whispered softly and woefully—
"We'll buy you some masses to scour away sin."
"And drink at my lyke-wake," quo' Tam o' the Lin.

THE WEE PICKLE TOW.

A lively young lass had a wee pickle tow,
    And she thought to try the spinning o't;
She sat by the fire, and the rock took a low,
    And that was an ill beginning o't.
Loud and shrill was the cry that she uttered, I ween :
The sudden mischanter brought tears to her e'en;
Her face it was fair, but her temper was keen.
    O dule for the ill beginning o't !

She stamp'd on the floor, and her twa hands she wrung;
    Her bonny sweet mou' she crookit O !
And fell was the outbreak o' words frae her tongue,
    Like ane sair demented she lookit O !
" Foul fa' the inventor o' rock and o' reel !
I hope, Gude forgie me, he's now wi' the deil;
He brought us mair trouble than help wot I weel.
    O dule for the ill beginning o't !

" And noo they are spinning and hemping awa',
    They'll talk o' my rock and the burning o't;
While Tibbie, and Mysie, and Maggie and a',
    Into some silly joke will be turning it.
They'll say I was doited, they'll say I was fou;
They'll say I was dowie and Robin untrue;
They'll say in the fire some love pouther I threw,
    And that made the ill beginning o't !

"Oh, curst be the day, and unchancy the hour,
  When I sat me a-down to the spinning o't!
Then some evil spirit or warlock had power,
  And made sic an ill beginning o't.
May spunkie my feet to the boggie betray,
The lunzie folk steal my new kirtle away,
And Robin forsake me for douce Effie Gray,
  The next time I try the spinning o't."

THE LOVER'S WATCH.

The gowan glitters on the sward,
  The laverock's in the sky,
And Colley on my plaid keeps ward,
  While time is passing by.
    Oh no! sad and slow!
    I hear nae welcome sound;
  The shadow of our trysting bush,
    It wears so slowly round!

My sheep-bell tinkles frae the west,
  My lambs are bleating near;
But still the sound that I lo'e best,
  Alack! I canna hear.
    Oh no! sad and slow,
    The shadow lingers still,
  And like a lanely ghaist I stand,
    And croon upon the hill. .

I hear below the water roar,
  The mill wi' clacking din,
And Lucky scolding frae her door,
  To ca' the bairnies in.
    Oh no! sad and slow!
    These are nae sounds for me;
  The shadow of our trysting bush,
    It creeps sae drearily!

I coft yestreen, frae chapman Tam,
  A snood of bonny blue,
And promised, when our trysting cam',
  To tie it round her brow.
    Oh no! sad and slow!
    The mark it winna pass;
  The shadow of that weary thorn
    Is tethered on the grass.

O now I see her on the way;
  She's past the witches' knowe;
She's climbing up the browny's brae,
  My heart is in a lowe!
    Oh no! 'tis not so!
    'Tis glaumerie I have seen;
  The shadow of that hawthorn bush
    Will move nae mair till e'en.

My book o' grace I'll try to read,
  Though conn'd wi' little skill:

When Colley barks I'll raise my head,
And find her on the hill.
Oh no! sad and slow,
The time will ne'er be gane;
The shadow of the trysting bush
Is fixed like ony stane.

POVERTY PARTS GOOD COMPANY.

When my o'erlay was white as the foam o' the lin,
And siller was chinkin' my pouches within,
When my lambkins were bleatin' on meadow and brae,
As I went to my love in new cleathing sae gay,
    Kind was she, and my friends were free,
    But poverty parts gude company.

How swift pass'd the minutes and hours of delight!
The piper played cheerie, the crusie burn'd bright,
And linked in my hand was the maiden sae dear,
As she footed the floor in her holiday gear!
    Woe's me! and can it then be
    That poverty parts sic company?

We met at the fair, and we met at the kirk;
We met in the sunshine, we met in the mirk;
And the sound o' her voice and the blinks o' her e'en,
The cheerin' and life of my bosom hae been.

Leaves frae the tree at Martinmas flee,
And poverty parts sweet company.

At bridal and infare I've braced me wi' pride,
The broose I hae won and a kiss o' the bride;
And loud was the laughter good fellows among,
As I uttered my banter or chorus'd my song.
    Dowie to dree are jestin' and glee,
    When poverty spoils gude company.

Wherever I gaed, kindly lasses looked sweet,
And mithers and aunties were unco discreet;
While kebbuck and bicker were set on the board;
But now they pass by me, and never a word.
    Sae let it be, for the worldly and slee
    Wi' poverty keep nae company.

But the hope o' my love is a cure for its smart,
And the spae-wife has tauld me to keep up my heart;
For wi' my last saxpence her loof I hae crost,
And the bliss that is fated can never be lost,
    Tho' cruelly we may ilka day see
    How poverty parts dear company.

"SAW YE JOHNNY COMIN'?"

"Saw ye Johnny comin'?" quo' she.
  "Saw ye Johnny comin'?
Wi' his blue bonnet on his head,
  And his doggie runnin'?
Yestreen, about the gloamin' time,
  I chanced to see him comin',
Whistling merrily the tune
  That I am a' day hummin'," quo' she,
"I am a' day hummin'."

"Fee him, faither, fee him," quo' she;
  "Fee him, faither, fee him;
A' the wark about the house
  Gaes wi' me when I see him.
A' the wark about the house
  I gang sae lightly through it;
And though ye pay some merks o' gear—
  Hoot! ye winna rue it," quo' she—
"Na, ye winna rue it."

"What wad I dae wi' him, Meggy?—
  What wad I dae him?
He's ne'er a sark upon his back,
  And I hae nane to gie him."

"I hae twa sarks into my kist,
  And ane o' them I'll gie him,
And for a merk o' mair fee
  O, dinna stand wi' him," quo' she—
"Dinna stand wi' him.

"Weel do I lo'e him," quo' she;
  "Weel do I lo'e him.
The brawest lads about the place
  Are a' but haverels to him.
O fee him, faither; lang, I trow,
  We've dull and dowie been;
He'll haud the plough, thrash i' the barn,
  And crack wi' me at e'en," quo' she—
"Crack wi' me at e'en."

THE END.

NEW BOOKS.

THE WINDOW; or, the Songs of the Wrens. A Song-Cycle by ALFRED TENNYSON, Poet Laureate, with Music by ARTHUR SULLIVAN. 4to cloth, gilt edges, 21s.

IONA. By the DUKE OF ARGYLL. With Illustrations. Crown 8vo, 3s. 6d.

ESSAYS, THEOLOGICAL AND LITERARY. By R. H. HUTTON. 2 vols. square 8vo, 24s.

DOROTHY FOX. By LOUISA PARR. 3 vols. post 8vo, 31s. 6d.

REHEARSALS; a Book of Verses. By J. LEICESTER WARREN, Author of "Philoctetes," etc. Crown 8vo, 6s.

EPISODES IN AN OBSCURE LIFE: a Curate's Experiences in the Tower Hamlets. 3 vols. post 8vo, 31s. 6d.

CHAMBER DRAMAS FOR CHILDREN. By MRS. GEORGE MACDONALD. Crown 8vo, 7s. 6d.

WALKS IN ROME. By AUGUSTUS J. C. HARE. 2 vols. crown 8vo, 21s.

AT THE BACK OF THE NORTH WIND. By GEORGE MACDONALD. With Illustrations by ARTHUR HUGHES. Crown 8vo, 7s. 6d.

KESHUB CHUNDER SEN'S ENGLISH VISIT. An Authorized Collection of his principal Addresses delivered in this Country. Edited by S. D. COLLET. Crown 8vo, 9s.

HALF-HOURS IN THE TEMPLE CHURCH. By C. J. VAUGHAN, D.D., Master of the Temple. Small 8vo, 3s. 6d.

PEEPS AT THE FAR EAST: a Familiar Account of a Visit to India. By NORMAN MACLEOD, D.D. With Illustrations. Small 4to, 16s.

SHOEMAKERS' VILLAGE. By HENRY HOLBEACH.
2 vols. crown 8vo.

THE SONGSTRESSES OF SCOTLAND. By
Misses TYTLER and WATSON. 2 vols. post 8vo, 24s.

THE BOY IN GREY. By HENRY KINGSLEY. With
Illustration by ARTHUR HUGHES. Crown 8vo, 3s. 6d.

JASMINE LEIGH. By C. FRASER TYTLER. Crown
8vo, 5s.

RANALD BANNERMAN'S BOYHOOD. By
GEORGE MACDONALD. With Illustrations by ARTHUR
HUGHES. Crown 8vo, 5s.

*REASONS FOR RETURNING TO THE
CHURCH OF ENGLAND.* Crown 8vo, 5s.

THE MIRACLES OF OUR LORD. By GEORGE
MACDONALD. Crown 8vo, 5s.

HEROINES IN OBSCURITY. A Second Series
of Papers for Thoughtful Girls. By SARAH TYTLER. Crown
8vo, 5s.

LECTURES AND TRACTS. By BABOO KESHUB
CHUNDER SEN. Edited by S. D. COLLET. Crown 8vo, 5s.

LILLIPUT LECTURES. By the Author of "Lilliput Levee." With Illustrations by ARTHUR HUGHES. Square
8vo, 5s.

GINX'S BABY; his Birth and other Misfortunes.
Seventh Edition. Crown 8vo, 5s.

EVENINGS AT THE TEA-TABLE. With Illustrations. Square 32mo, 3s. 6d.

THE COMPANIONS OF ST. PAUL. By J. S.
HOWSON, D.D., Dean of Chester. Crown 8vo, 5s.

NAPOLEON FALLEN: a Lyrical Drama. By ROBERT BUCHANAN. Second Edition. Crown 8vo, 3s. 6d.

STRAHAN & CO., 56, LUDGATE HILL.

www.ingramcontent.com/pod-product-compliance
Lightning Source LLC
Chambersburg PA
CBHW032050220426
43664CB00008B/942